THE F...
TRIL...

Blood Wedding,
Yerma, and
...rda Alba

THE RURAL TRILOGY

Blood Wedding, Yerma, and The House of Bernarda Alba

Federico García Lorca

A New English Translation by Michael Dewell and Carmen Zapata

Introduction by Douglas Day

BANTAM BOOKS
TORONTO · NEW YORK · LONDON · SYDNEY · AUCKLAND

THE RURAL TRILOGY
A *Bantam Book* / *September 1987*

Book design by Nicola Mazzella.

Library of Congress Cataloging-in-Publication Data

García Lorca, Federico, 1898-1936.
   The rural trilogy.

   I. Title.
PQ6613.A763A226   1987   862'.62   87-47559
ISBN 0-553-34434-X

Published simultaneously in the United States and Canada

PRINTED IN THE UNITED STATES OF AMERICA

FG   0 9 8 7 6 5 4 3 2 1

The translators dedicate their work to:

Margarita Galban
   —for asking them to do it,

Nina Foch
   —for believing they could,

The Del Amo Foundation
   —for getting them started.

ABOUT THE TRANSLATORS

MICHAEL DEWELL is president of the National Repertory Theatre Foundation, for which he has produced a range of works by playwrights from Euripedes to Arthur Miller. His productions have toured nationally and played on Broadway, winning many awards including a special "Tony" for distinguished contribution to the American Theatre. In 1968, Dewell and NRT reopened Ford's Theatre in Washington for the federal government. He has written numerous articles on theatre for newspapers and national magazines.

Carmen Zapata is president of the Bilingual Foundation of the Arts, an Hispanic-American theatre in Los Angeles which tours California, the Middle West, and has twice played New York—at Lincoln Center and at the Public Theatre. For BFA, she has produced fifty-one plays in English and Spanish over the past fourteen years. Best known as an actress familiar to film and television audiences around the country, she also serves on the California Council for the Humanities, teaches for UCLA extension, and lectures widely.

CONTENTS

ﻼﻼﻼ

INTRODUCTION

⧫⧫⧫

A critic once wrote that "thematically, García Lorca's theater revolves on a single axis: *the preservation of Honor leads to the frustration of love, hence of life itself; this frustration, in turn, becomes a despair which leads to Death.* This is always the major theme. . . ."[1] Is Lorca, Spain's greatest modern writer, to be circumscribed so easily? The answer, somewhat to our surprise, is yes, especially when we concentrate on his three splendid folk tragedies, *Bodas de Sangre* (1933), *Yerma* (1934), and *La Casa de Bernarda Alba* (1936). As a thinker, Lorca was swift and agile, but not deep. He didn't try to be, and he didn't need to be. During his years at the Residencia de Estudiantes in Madrid, he seldom attended lectures. Instead, he would ask friends like Salvador Dali and Luis Buñuel to tell him about the lectures. People told him what he might have gotten from books he hadn't read.

This is not to say that Lorca was a lazy, shallow man or that his great works, like the three tragedies, or *El Llanto por Ignacio Sánchez Mejías,* his long elegy to a dead matador, or his final, ferocious collection of poems, *El Diván del Tamarit,* lack depth: far from it. Their depths belong to things much harder than mere ideas for a critic to extract. To get to Lorca, one must be prepared to search for words that lie in that place where the tangible meets the intangible, that realm where air, song, love, earth, water, hatred all meet at once—and where death is both blossom and root of the exotic Sephirotic Tree Lorca considered existence to be.

In fact, Lorca distrusted words, especially when set down to be read. He always considered himself a *juglar,* Andalusian anteced-

---

[1]Robert Lima, *The Theater of García Lorca* (New York, 1963), p. 291.

ent to the Provençal jongleur or minstrel. He was happiest when he was singing his poems to his friends in his raspy but hypnotic voice (like that of an old flamenco *cantaor*, harsh from cognac and black-tobacco cigarettes) or chanting his plays to them in a manner either sprightly or doom-laden, as the dialogue required. He never read his work; he performed it, sometimes accompanying himself on guitar, sometimes swaying sinuously about on his imaginary stage.

For most of his career, his friends had almost to force him to publish his poems, to produce his plays. He was, unlike Yeats for example, indifferent to "correct" texts or definitive versions. He was after immediate and startling effects, not scholarship. Typically, he would sing a poem he had just composed, write it out casually on the back of an envelope, forget about it, then publish it years later as he best remembered it.

More important than his attitude toward his writing, though, was the emotional intensity Lorca wanted his work to possess. What he was after in these plays, as in his earlier poetry collections, *Romancero Gitano* (1928) and *Poema del Cante Jondo* (composed in 1921, but not published until 1931), was *cante jondo*, deep song, the darkest, most solemn form of what we loosely call flamenco, that ancient music that expressed for Lorca the soul of his Andalucía. When, late at night in a gathering of *cantaores* and *tocaores*, the wailing and lamenting reached their peak, a kind of frisson would run through the room where the performance was being given—so that the music produced that overdescribed and misunderstood thing called *duende*. In one of his infrequent lectures ("Play and Theory of the Duende," 1931), Lorca cited his friend, the Gypsy *cantaor* Manuel Torre, as saying "All that has black sounds has *duende*," and then went on to explain:

> These black sounds are the mystery, the roots fastened into the mire that we all know, that we all ignore, but where we reach what is deepest in art. . . . Thus, the *duende* is a power and not a work, a struggle and not a thought. I have heard an

old maestro of the guitar say, "*Duende* is not in the throat; *duende* climbs up inside you, from the bottom of your feet." Meaning this: it is not a question of ability, but of true, living style, of blood, of the most ancient culture, of spontaneous creation.

This *duende* may arise not only in music, but also in the bull-fight, when the matador is inspired to work his art with a genius he doesn't really possess, or when love and death and earth mix with such pain (the *pena negra*, the Gypsies call it) that the cry of *duende* is— as Lorca says in another essay—sharp enough to split the quicksilver from a mirror.

Now, for Lorca to write these three tragedies with the aim of conjuring up the black sounds, the *duende*, not only among the characters on stage but also within the audience itself, has little to do with what most of us today think of as "theater." We do have our avant-garde, which has its premise that we are all sophisti-cates, performing a sort of aesthetic gymnastics for the evening, and we allow a certain amount of fantasy and horror, but we must admit that most of our expectations for drama lie somewhere in the realm of the mimetic. Chthonic, shattering passion such as one finds in Lorca is too strong—even a little embarrassing. Over-wrought, melodramatic, one might say. Or one might begin to realize that these plays are closer to opera than to "theater."

Lorca is sui generis. He has few antecedents, though attempts are made occasionally to link him with Maeterlinck, Yeats, or Synge. Of these, only Synge's plays connect with Lorca's trage-dies. The first two playwrights may relate in various ways to Lor-ca's other, more surrealistic, more literarily "poetic" plays like *Asi que Pasen Cinco Anos* (1929-1930) or *El Público* (begun in 1930, and never completed or produced). Among his countrymen, only Ramón del Valle-Inclán comes close. And no one comes after him—except for a host of Anglo-American critics and reviewers, all of whom seem to begin their essays by writing, "The trouble with Lorca . . . ."

The trouble with Lorca, here, is that—for us Anglos, at least—

his tragedies are overcharged with emotion. And with daring. He uses the conventional structure of drama (three acts, so many scenes, and so on), and he sets little traps for us to make us think that we are with him in a land that is foreign but recognizable. A note at the beginning of Lorca's original version of *La Casa de Bernarda Alba,* for instance, announces, "The writer states that these three acts are intended as a photographic document." So we believe that our expectations are going to be met: we are going to see a play about peasants in Andalucía and the harsh lives they lead.

In fact, each of the tragedies came to Lorca from the world we call "real." *Bodas de Sangre* derives from Lorca's fascination with a momentarily famous crime of passion that took place in the countryside near Níjar, in the southeastern province of Almería, in the summer of 1928. A bride had, on the day of her wedding, run off with her cousin. The bridegroom had followed them, and the two men had killed each other. After his fashion, Lorca thought about this for four years, then—without having made so much as an outline—wrote the play in one week.

For *Yerma,* Lorca thought of the annual spring pilgrimage to Moclín, a mountain village northwest of his Granada. Every year, barren wives and their shamefaced husbands made the climb to Moclín, where all manner of pious ritual and impious coupling went on. ("*Ay, que cachondeo!*" an old aunt of Lorca's exclaimed to me when I asked her about Moclín. *Cachondeo* doesn't translate well; but "What a horny time!" might do.)

And Lorca had ample opportunity to learn at first hand about the house of Bernarda Alba. She and her daughters lived next door to the Lorca family for several years in Fuentevaqueros, the town near Granada where Lorca was born, and (so the story goes) the adolescent Lorca would hide on the wall separating the patios of the two houses and watch the goings-on of the vicious widow and her embittered daughters.

Partly because of this basis (however spurious or exaggerated) in a "real" world, the tragedies are indeed deceptive. Of course we expect Lorca to rearrange, modify, and select the facts of the

Níjar case in composing *Bodas de Sangre*, and this he does do. And there is nothing very surprising about his introducing a very old, very famous *nana*, a lullaby, at the opening of Act I, Scene 2:

Sleep, my child, and dream
About the giant horse
Who didn't want the water.

But when we read on and see how Lorca has modified the lullaby to include references to a silver dagger and to blood flowing faster than water and how he has allowed the mother-in-law to say to the horse:

Go off to the mountain
Through the grey valleys,
Where the mare waits,

we realize that he is using his little lament to tell us in coded form what the plot of the play will become. Leonardo, the stallion, will ride over the mountains to the grey valley where the bride lives. She is a stream from which he cannot drink, and his life will end with a silver dagger. (Silver always connotes death in Lorca.) The single theme that my critic defined so well on the first page of this introduction is working its way along, but throughout the play Lorca pays as much attention to color, music, and choreography (and flowers: think of the bridegroom's *waxen* orange blossoms, his wedding gift to the bride) as he does to methodically working out the plot.

But there is still nothing too unusual or startling about this sort of poetic symbolism. It is not until we come to the beginning of Act III in the improbably tropical (and phallic) forest where Leonardo and the bride have hidden, and we encounter the three woodcutters who speak to the accompaniment of two violins, that we realize Lorca has been leading us up to the wild cries of deep song. The Moon (a young woodcutter with a silver face) comes in to foretell the couple's doom. Then Death itself, in the person of an old Beggar Woman, enters to lead the bridegroom to the place where his betrayers are hidden. From now until the end of this stunning scene, when we hear the twin shrieks of the young men as they die, Lorca is pulling us as far as he can into "the mire that we all know, that we all ignore, but where we reach what is deepest in art." And with the final, contrapuntal dialogue between the bridegroom's mother and his virgin widow, we come as close to real *duende* as anything that is not true *cante jondo* can come:

> With a knife, with a little knife
> That . . . penetrates precisely
> Through the astonished flesh
> To stop exactly at the place
> Where, trembling and entangled,
> Lies the dark root of the stream.

This is poetry, all right, but it is not "poetic drama"—not, that is, if by poetic drama we mean T. S. Eliot or Christopher Fry. It is more like the poetry of an old flamenco *letra* that goes:

> When they put my mother
> In her grave
> I covered her face with a handkerchief
> So the earth would not fall in her mouth.

In *Yerma*, too, there is a fatal triangle: Yerma, the barren woman, strangles her feckless husband, Juan, while Victor, the shepherd whom nature intended as her mate, stands forlornly out in the fields with his sheep. By classical definitions and by its theme (the same theme always), *Yerma* is indeed a tragedy; but there is a strange tenderness throughout the play to remind us that Lorca could write not only with and about frustration and violence, but also about such things as the way a pregnant woman feels: "Haven't you ever had a live bird held tight in your hand?" Or about the anguish of a barren woman in a peasant culture: "Why am I barren? Am I going to spend my best years feeding

birds and hanging starched curtains in my window? No! You must
tell me what I have to do, and I'll do whatever it is, even if you
make me stick needles in the most sensitive parts of my eyes!"

But the poignancy and lyricism gradually yield to true bitterness and despair as the years pass, and Yerma turns savage in her
frenzied attempts to find a way to become pregnant by Juan (it
must be Juan, her husband, because Yerma is an honorable
woman). At the pilgrimage to Moclín that I mentioned earlier,
Lorca gives us two of his most brilliant pageants: one is a pious
procession of women who go in penitence to pray for fecundity;
the other is a scene of what Lorca himself calls "great beauty and
earthiness." This is a ceremonial pagan fertility dance, involving
archetypal male and female figures (Lorca calls them *Macho* and
Hembra), and the author leaves little room to doubt that he pre-
fers the latter ceremony to the former. But it is all too late for
Yerma; it has been too late since the day she married Juan. She
ends by standing over Juan's body, screaming at the crowd that is
gathering:

> What do you want to know? Don't come near me, for I have
> killed my son! I myself have killed my son!

In *Yerma*, as throughout most of Lorca's work, it is the woman
who gets his sympathy; his men are generally there either to tor-
ment his women or to stand vapidly by as the brutal action unfolds against the woman. Woman suffers; man inflicts suffering.
Man, or his institutions, like the Church. Or his ideas, like Honor,
and Respectability.

So it should come as no surprise that in the last of his plays, *La
Casa de Bernarda Alba*, the women are imprisoned, practically
speaking forever, by a woman who, all femininity driven from her
by a lifetime spent in a world that men and the Church and an
inverted sense of honor have built, rages at her five daughters.
The walls of the house are white. The women wear black. There
is only one other color in the play: the green dress that Adela, the
youngest daughter, wears as her way of defying the awful mother.

Except for the mad, pathetic songs of Bernarda's ancient mother, there is no music in this play, no poetry. As Wilfred Owen said, "The poetry is in the pity." If there is pity in this play, it must be that which the audience feels for the characters, for they feel almost none for themselves. It is almost as if Lorca had said to himself: "Write about hatred. Write about what makes women hate." And hate they do, more than any characters since the Revenge Tragedies of the sixteenth century; so much so that by the time we reach the last scene, we are not even too appalled at hearing Martirio, one of the sisters, say of Adela: "I'd like to pour a river of blood over her head!" Adela finally hangs herself, and we end with the spectacle of an old woman in black demanding silence in a room in which there is no sound at all (and where there will never be a sound) and crying out in defiance to the world that her daughter died a virgin.

There is no starker drama than this. This is what *cante jondo* can come to, if it is true enough, felt strongly enough: the dancer and the guitarist cease, and there is left only the hopeless wail of the bereft singer. Lorca succeeded: a superior performance (or a careful reading) will arouse the spirit of *duende*. A few months after completing *La Casa de Bernarda Alba* he was dead, assassinated in the hills above Granada. He left fragments of new plays, but we have no way of knowing whether or not he could have surpassed his last one. I think not.

DOUGLAS DAY
THE UNIVERSITY OF VIRGINIA

BLOOD WEDDING

∽∽∽

BLOOD WEDDING

⋙⋙⋙

Cast of Characters

BRIDEGROOM
MOTHER
NEIGHBOR
MOTHER-IN-LAW
WIFE
LEONARDO
GIRL
MAID
FATHER
BRIDE
FIRST GIRL
SECOND GIRL

THIRD GIRL
FIRST YOUNG MAN
SECOND YOUNG MAN
FIRST YOUTH
FIRST WOODCUTTER
SECOND WOODCUTTER
THIRD WOODCUTTER
MOON
BEGGAR WOMAN
YOUNG GIRL
LITTLE GIRL

ACT I

৩৽৩

SCENE 1

The room is painted yellow.

BRIDEGROOM: Mother?

MOTHER: Yes?

BRIDEGROOM: I'm going.

MOTHER: Where?

BRIDEGROOM: To the vineyard. *(He starts to go.)*

MOTHER: Wait.

BRIDEGROOM: Do you need something?

MOTHER: Son, your breakfast!

BRIDEGROOM: Never mind. I'll eat some grapes. Give me the knife.

MOTHER: What for?

BRIDEGROOM: To cut them with.

MOTHER: The knife! The knife! Damn all of them! *And* the monster who invented them!

BRIDEGROOM: Let's change the subject.

MOTHER: And the shotguns and the pistols and the smallest knife—and even the pitchfork and the hoe!

BRIDEGROOM: Enough!

MOTHER: Anything that can cut into a man's body! A beautiful man, with life like a flower in his mouth, who goes out to his

5

vineyards or to his own olive groves, because they are his, inherited . . .

BRIDEGROOM: Mother, be quiet!

MOTHER: . . . and that man does not return. Or if he does, it's only to have a palm placed over him—or a dish of rock salt so his body won't swell. I don't know how you dare to carry a knife on you! Or why I allow this serpent inside the cupboard!

BRIDEGROOM: Haven't you said enough?

MOTHER: If I lived a hundred years, I would talk of nothing else! First, your father. To me, he smelled like carnations, and I enjoyed him only three short years. Then your brother. Is it fair? How can it be that something as small as a pistol or a knife can destroy a man who is like a bull? I'll never be quiet. The months go by, and the desperation stings my eyes and the very tips of my hair!

BRIDEGROOM: Are we going to stop this?

MOTHER: No, we're not going to stop this! Can anyone bring me back your father? Or your brother? And then there is the prison. What is a prison? People eat there, they smoke there, they play their music there. My dead ones, covered with weeds, silent, turned to dust. Two men who were like two geraniums! The killers—in prison, cool, gazing at the mountains.

BRIDEGROOM: Do you want me to kill them?

MOTHER: No. . . . If I talk about it, it's because— How can I *not* talk about it, watching you go out that door? I don't want you to carry a knife. I just . . . I just wish you wouldn't go out to the fields.

BRIDEGROOM: (*laughing*) Mother!

MOTHER: How I wish you had been a girl! You wouldn't be going out to the vineyard now. And we would be embroidering linens and little wool dogs.

BRIDEGROOM: (*takes her by the arm and laughs*) Mother, what if I take you with me to the vineyard?

MOTHER: What would an old woman be doing in the vineyard! Would you hide me under the vine leaves?

BRIDEGROOM: *(lifting her up in his arms)* Old woman! Old, old woman! Old, old, old woman!

MOTHER: Your father himself used to take me. That's good stock, good blood! Your grandfather left a son in every corner. That I like—men that are men, wheat that is wheat.

BRIDEGROOM: And me, Mother?

MOTHER: What about you?

BRIDEGROOM: Do I have to tell you again?

MOTHER: *(serious)* Oh!

BRIDEGROOM: Does it bother you?

MOTHER: No.

BRIDEGROOM: What is it?

MOTHER: I don't know myself. Suddenly, like this, it always surprises me. I know she's a good girl. That's true, isn't it? Well-mannered, hard-working. She bakes her bread and sews her dresses—and yet, every time I mention her, I feel as if I'd been struck in the forehead with a rock.

BRIDEGROOM: That's nonsense!

MOTHER: It's not nonsense. I'll be left alone! You're all I have now, and it makes me sad that you'll be leaving.

BRIDEGROOM: But you will come with us.

MOTHER: No. I can't leave your father and your brother alone here. I have to go there every morning. And if I go away, one of the Felixes might easily die. One of that family of killers! And they could bury him right next to them. And that—never! Never! Because I will dig him up with my fingernails! And all by myself, I will smash him against the wall!

BRIDEGROOM: *(loudly)* Back to that again!

MOTHER: Forgive me. *(pause)* How long have you been seeing her?

BRIDEGROOM: Three years. I was finally able to buy the vineyard.

MOTHER: Three years. She used to see someone else, didn't she?

BRIDEGROOM: I don't know—I don't think so. Girls have to look carefully at who they are going to marry.

MOTHER: Yes . . . I didn't look at anyone. I looked at your father, and when they killed him, I looked at the wall in front of me. One woman with one man, and that's it.

BRIDEGROOM: You know she's a good girl.

MOTHER: I don't doubt it. Anyway, it's too bad I don't know what her mother was like.

BRIDEGROOM: Does it matter?

MOTHER: *(looking at him)* Son!

BRIDEGROOM: What do you want?

MOTHER: It's true! You're right! When do you want me to ask for her?

BRIDEGROOM: *(happily)* Would Sunday be all right?

MOTHER: I'll take her those brass earrings, they're antiques. And you buy her—

BRIDEGROOM: You know more—

MOTHER: —buy her some lace stockings. And for yourself, two suits. No, three! You're all I have now.

BRIDEGROOM: I'm leaving. Tomorrow, I'll go to see her.

MOTHER: Yes. Yes. And try to please me with six grandchildren— or as many as you feel like, since your father had no chance to give me any more children of my own.

BRIDEGROOM: The first will be for you.

MOTHER: Yes. But have some girls! I want to embroider, and make lace, and be at peace.

BRIDEGROOM: I'm sure you will love her.

MOTHER: I will love her. *(She starts to kiss him, but draws back.)* Go on. You're too old for kisses. Give them to your wife. *(She pauses. Then, to herself)* When she *is* your wife.

BRIDEGROOM: I'm leaving.

MOTHER: You better hoe the vines over by the little mill. You've been neglecting them.

BRIDEGROOM: Whatever you say.

MOTHER: God go with you.

(The BRIDEGROOM exits. The MOTHER remains seated, with her back to the door. A NEIGHBOR wearing a dark dress and a scarf on her head appears at the door.)

MOTHER: Welcome.

NEIGHBOR: How are you?

MOTHER: As you see.

NEIGHBOR: I came down to the store and dropped in to see you. We live so far apart!

MOTHER: It's been twenty years since I've climbed to the top of that street.

NEIGHBOR: You seem well.

MOTHER: You think so?

NEIGHBOR: Things happen. Two days ago they brought in my neighbor's son—with both his arms cut off by the machine. *(She sits.)*

MOTHER: Rafael?

NEIGHBOR: Yes. And there you have it. Many times I think your son and mine are better off where they are—asleep, resting, and not in danger of being left useless.

MOTHER: Don't say that. That's all just talk, but it's no consolation.

NEIGHBOR: *(She sighs.)*

MOTHER: *(She sighs.)*

(There is a moment of silence.)

NEIGHBOR: *(sadly)* Where is your boy?

MOTHER: He's out.

NEIGHBOR: He finally bought the vineyard!

MOTHER: He was fortunate.

NEIGHBOR: And now he will get married.

MOTHER: *(As if suddenly roused, she draws her chair nearer to that of her* NEIGHBOR.*)* Listen!

NEIGHBOR: *(confidentially)* Yes?

MOTHER: Do you know this girl my son wants to marry?

NEIGHBOR: A good girl!

MOTHER: Yes, but . . .

NEIGHBOR: But there is no one who *really* knows her. She lives there alone with her father, so far away—fifteen miles from the

nearest house. But she's a good girl, accustomed to being
alone.

MOTHER: What about her mother?

NEIGHBOR: Her mother, I *did* know. She was beautiful! Her face
shone like a saint's. But I never liked her. She didn't love her
husband.

MOTHER: *(firmly)* The things some people seem to know!

NEIGHBOR: Pardon me! I didn't mean to offend you, but it's true.
Now whether or not she was a decent woman, no one said.
There's been no talk about that. She acted so superior.

MOTHER: Always the same!

NEIGHBOR: You asked me.

MOTHER: I just wish that no one knew either the one who's dead
or the one who's alive—that they were like two thistles that
would prick any wagging tongue that touched them.

NEIGHBOR: You're right. Your son deserves the best.

MOTHER: The best. That's why I take care of him. . . . I was told
the girl was engaged to another man, some time ago.

NEIGHBOR: She must have been fifteen years old. He got married
two years ago—to one of her cousins, as a matter of fact. No
one remembers that engagement.

MOTHER: How is it *you* remember?

NEIGHBOR: You ask me such questions!

MOTHER: Each of us wants to find out what can hurt us. Who was
he?

NEIGHBOR: Leonardo.

MOTHER: Leonardo who?

NEIGHBOR: Leonardo Felix.

MOTHER: Felix!

NEIGHBOR: How could anything be Leonardo's fault? He was
eight years old at the time it happened.

MOTHER: That's true. But I just hear—Felix! *(between her
teeth)*—and hearing "Felix" is like having my mouth fill up
with slime! *(She spits.)* And I have to spit! I have to spit so I
won't kill!

NEIGHBOR: Control yourself! What do you gain from this?

MOTHER: Nothing. But you do understand.

NEIGHBOR: Don't stand in the way of your son's happiness. Don't say anything to him. You're an old woman. So am I. For you and me, it is time to be quiet.

MOTHER: I will say nothing to him.

NEIGHBOR: *(kissing her)* Nothing.

MOTHER: *(calmly)* Such things . . .

NEIGHBOR: I'm leaving. My people will be coming in from the fields soon.

MOTHER: Have you ever seen such a hot day?

NEIGHBOR: The children who take water out to the reapers are black from the sun. Good-bye, my friend.

MOTHER: Good-bye.

CURTAIN

ACT I

⨯⨯⨯

SCENE 2

The room is painted pink, with kitchen furniture and bunches of everyday flowers. At center, a table with a tablecloth. It is morning. LEONARDO's MOTHER-IN-LAW *holds a* CHILD *in her arms. She rocks him. The* WIFE *sits in a corner, embroidering.*

MOTHER-IN-LAW:
    Sleep, my child, and dream
    About the giant horse
    Who didn't want the water.
    The water, deep and black,
    In among the branches.
    Arriving at the bridge,
    The water stops and sings.
    Who can say, my child,
    What the water holds?
    —With its flowing tail,
    Along its verdant hall.
WIFE: *(softly)*
    Go to sleep, my flower—
    The horse does not want water.
MOTHER-IN-LAW:
    Go to sleep, my rose—

12

The horse begins to cry.
His wounded hooves,
His frozen mane,
And in his eyes,
A silver dagger.
They went to the river,
Down to the river!
The blood was flowing
Faster than water.

WIFE:
Go to sleep, my flower—
The horse does not want water.

MOTHER-IN-LAW:
Go to sleep, my rose—
The horse is beginning to cry.

WIFE:
He would not touch
The riverside.
His mouth was hot
With silver flies.
Alone, he cried out
To the cruel mountains,
With the dead river
Around his throat.
The giant horse
Did not want water!
The sorrow of snow,
The horse of the dawn.

MOTHER-IN-LAW:
Stay back! Don't come!
Close the window
With branches of dreams
And dreams of branches.

WIFE:
My child is sleeping.

MOTHER-IN-LAW:
   My child is quiet.
WIFE:
   O Horse, my child
   Has a pillow,
MOTHER-IN-LAW:
   His cradle of steel,
WIFE:
   His blanket of linen.
MOTHER-IN-LAW:
   Sleep, my child, and dream.
WIFE:
   Oh, the giant horse
   Who did not want the water!
MOTHER-IN-LAW:
   Don't come! Don't enter!
   Go off to the mountain
   Through the grey valleys,
   Where the mare waits.
WIFE:
   My child is sleeping.
MOTHER-IN-LAW:
   My child is resting.
WIFE: *(softly)*
   Go to sleep, my flower—
   The horse does not want water.
MOTHER-IN-LAW: *(rising, very softly)*
   Go to sleep, my rose—
   The horse is beginning to cry.

(MOTHER-IN-LAW *exits with* CHILD. LEONARDO *enters.*)

LEONARDO: Where's the child?
WIFE: He's sleeping.
LEONARDO: He wasn't well yesterday. He cried during the night.

WIFE: Today he's like a dahlia. What about you? Have you been to the blacksmith?

LEONARDO: I just came from there. Can you believe that for more than two months I've been putting new shoes on that horse, and they keep coming off? He must be tearing them off on the rocks.

WIFE: Could it be you ride him too much?

LEONARDO: No. I hardly use him at all.

WIFE: Yesterday, the neighbors told me they had seen you at the far end of the flats.

LEONARDO: Who said that?

WIFE: The women who were out gathering capers. It certainly surprised me. Was it you?

LEONARDO: No. What would I be doing out there in that desert?

WIFE: That's what I said. But the horse was drowning in sweat.

LEONARDO: Did you see it?

WIFE: No. My mother did.

LEONARDO: Is she with the child?

WIFE: Yes. Would you like some lemonade?

LEONARDO: With very cold water.

WIFE: Why didn't you come home to eat?

LEONARDO: I was with the wheat buyers. That always takes time.

WIFE: (*Making his drink, she speaks tenderly.*) Are they paying a good price?

LEONARDO: A fair one.

WIFE: I need a dress, and the baby needs a bonnet with bows.

LEONARDO: I'm going in to see him. (*He gets up.*)

WIFE: Be careful—he's asleep.

MOTHER-IN-LAW: (*as she enters*) Who rides that horse so hard? He's stretched out down there with his eyes rolling around, as if he'd come from the end of the earth.

LEONARDO: (*acidly*) Me.

MOTHER-IN-LAW: Pardon me! He *is* yours!

WIFE: He was with the wheat buyers.

MOTHER-IN-LAW: He can stay with them for all I care!

WIFE: Your lemonade—is it cold?

LEONARDO: Yes.

WIFE: Did you know they are asking for my cousin's hand?

LEONARDO: When?

WIFE: Tomorrow. The wedding will be within the month. I suppose they will be coming to invite us.

LEONARDO: I don't know.

MOTHER-IN-LAW: I don't think his mother was very happy about the marriage.

LEONARDO: And perhaps she is right. You have to watch out for her.

WIFE: I don't like you to think badly of a nice girl.

MOTHER-IN-LAW: But he says that because he knows her. Don't you realize they were seeing each other for three years?

LEONARDO: But I stopped seeing her! *(to his* WIFE) Are you going to cry now? Stop it! *(He brusquely pulls her hands away from her face.)* Let's go see the child.

(They exit, arms around each other. A GIRL *runs in, joyously.)*

GIRL: *Señora!*

MOTHER-IN-LAW: What is it?

GIRL: The bridegroom came to the store, and he's bought the best of everything there!

MOTHER-IN-LAW: Did he come by himself?

GIRL: No, with his mother—tall, dignified. *(She imitates her.)* And what finery!

MOTHER-IN-LAW: They have money.

GIRL: And they bought some lace stockings. Oh, what stockings! Women dream of such stockings! Look: A swallow here *(she points to her ankle)*, a boat here *(she points to her calf)*, and here *(she points to her thigh)*—a rose!

MOTHER-IN-LAW: Child!

GIRL: A rose with the seeds and the stem! Oh, and all done in silk!

MOTHER-IN-LAW: Two wealthy families are going to be joined.

(LEONARDO *and his* WIFE *enter.*)

GIRL: I came to tell you what they're buying.
LEONARDO: We don't care!
WIFE: Leave her alone.
MOTHER-IN-LAW: Leonardo, don't make so much of it!
GIRL: Please excuse me. *(She leaves, weeping.)*
MOTHER-IN-LAW: Why do you find it necessary to antagonize people?
LEONARDO: I didn't ask for your opinion.
MOTHER-IN-LAW: Very well!

(There is a pause.)

WIFE: What is wrong with you? What scheme is boiling up inside your head? Don't leave me this way—not knowing anything—
LEONARDO: Stop it!
WIFE: No. I want you to look at me and tell me.
LEONARDO: Leave me alone. *(He gets up.)*
WIFE: Where are you going?
LEONARDO: Will you be quiet?
MOTHER-IN-LAW: *(resolutely, to her daughter)* Shhh! (LEONARDO *exits.*) The child!

(She exits, and comes back with the CHILD *in her arms. The* WIFE *remains standing, motionless.)*

WIFE:
   His wounded hooves,
   His frozen mane,
   And in his eyes,
   A silver dagger.
MOTHER-IN-LAW:
   They went to the river,
   Down to the river!

The blood was flowing
Faster than water.

WIFE: *(turning slowly, as if in a dream)*
Go to sleep, my flower,
The horse is beginning to drink.

MOTHER-IN-LAW:
Go to sleep, my rose.
The horse is beginning to cry.

WIFE:
Sleep, my child, and dream.

MOTHER-IN-LAW:
Oh, the giant horse,
Who did not want the water!

WIFE: *(dramatically)*
Don't come! Don't enter!
Go off to the mountain.
Oh, sorrow of snow,
Horse of the dawn.

MOTHER-IN-LAW: *(weeping)*
My child is sleeping.

WIFE: *(weeping as she slowly moves closer)*
My child is resting.

MOTHER-IN-LAW:
Go to sleep, my flower.
The horse is beginning to drink.

WIFE: *(weeping, supporting herself on the table)*
Go to sleep, my rose.
The horse is beginning to cry.

CURTAIN

ACT I

∽◦∽◦∽

SCENE 3

Interior of the cave where the BRIDE *lives. Upstage, a cross of large, pink flowers. The archway doors have lace curtains tied with pink bows. On the white masonry walls are open fans, blue mugs, and small mirrors. The* BRIDEGROOM *and his* MOTHER *enter. The* MOTHER *is dressed in black satin and wears a lace mantilla. The* BRIDEGROOM *wears a black corduroy suit and a large gold chain.*

MAID: (*affably, full of hypocritical humility*) Come in. Would you like to sit down? They'll be right here.

(*She exits.* MOTHER *and* BRIDEGROOM *remain seated, as immobile as statues. A long pause.*)

MOTHER: Did you bring the watch?
BRIDEGROOM: Yes. (*He takes it out and looks at it.*)
MOTHER: We have to get back in time. How far away these people live!
BRIDEGROOM: But the land here is good.
MOTHER: Good, but much too lonely. Four hours on the road, and not a house or a tree!
BRIDEGROOM: This is a desert.

MOTHER: Your father would have covered it with trees.

BRIDEGROOM: Without water?

MOTHER: He would have found it. The three years he was married to me, he planted ten cherry trees, *(reminiscing)* the three walnuts by the mill, one whole vineyard, and a plant called Jupiter with blood-red flowers, and it died. *(pause)*

BRIDEGROOM: She must be getting dressed.

(The BRIDE's FATHER *enters—an elderly man with shining white hair. His head is inclined. The* MOTHER *and the* BRIDEGROOM *stand to shake hands silently.)*

FATHER: Was it a long journey?

MOTHER: Four hours. *(They sit down.)*

FATHER: You must have come the long way.

MOTHER: I am too old now to walk along the cliffs by the river.

BRIDEGROOM: She gets dizzy.

(Pause.)

FATHER: A good hemp harvest.

BRIDEGROOM: Truly good.

FATHER: In my time, not even hemp would grow on this land. You had to punish it, even cry over it, before it would provide us with something.

MOTHER: But now, it does. Don't complain—I didn't come to ask you for anything.

FATHER: *(smiling)* You are richer than I am. Your vineyards are worth a fortune. Each young vine, a silver coin! I'm only sorry that our lands—you understand?—are separated. I like everything together. There's one thorn in my heart, and it's that little orchard stuck right in the middle of my property. They won't sell it to me for all the gold in the world.

BRIDEGROOM: It's always that way.

FATHER: If we could take twenty teams of oxen and bring your vineyards over here and put them on the hillside— What joy!

MOTHER: What for?

FATHER: What's mine is hers, and what's yours is his, that's why! To see it all together. Because together is beautiful.

BRIDEGROOM: And it would be less work.

MOTHER: When I die, you can sell that place and buy next to this one.

FATHER: Sell? Sell! Bah! Buy, my dear, buy it all! If I had sons, I would have bought this whole mountain, as far as the river. It's not good land, but with muscle you make it good. And since people don't come this way, they don't steal your crops, and you can sleep peacefully.

MOTHER: *(after a pause)* You know why I've come?

FATHER: Yes.

MOTHER: Well?

FATHER: I think it's fine. They have talked it over.

MOTHER: My son is rich and capable.

FATHER: My daughter, too.

MOTHER: My son is beautiful. He has never known a woman. His reputation is cleaner than a sheet spread out in the sun.

FATHER: What can I tell you about my daughter? She makes bread at three o'clock while the morning star is still shining. She never talks—soft as wool. She embroiders all kinds of embroidery. And she can cut through a rope with her teeth.

MOTHER: God bless your house!

FATHER: May God bless it.

(The MAID *enters with two trays—one with wine glasses, the other with sweets.)*

MOTHER: *(to* BRIDEGROOM*)* When do you want the wedding?

BRIDEGROOM: Next Thursday.

FATHER: The day on which she will be exactly twenty-two years old.

MOTHER: Twenty-two years old. That would be the age of my

eldest son, if he were alive. And how alive he'd be—warm and manly as he was!—if men hadn't invented knives!

FATHER: One shouldn't think about that.

MOTHER: Every minute. Look into your own heart.

FATHER: Thursday, then. Isn't that right?

BRIDEGROOM: That's right.

FATHER: The bride and groom and the two of us will go to church in the carriage, since it's so far. And the wedding party in their own carts and on their own horses.

MOTHER: Agreed.

(The MAID enters.)

FATHER: Tell her that she can come in now. *(to the MOTHER)* I'll be very pleased if you like her.

(The BRIDE enters modestly, with folded hands and lowered head.)

MOTHER: Come closer. Are you happy?

BRIDE: Yes, *Señora.*

FATHER: You shouldn't look so serious. When all is said and done, she's going to be your mother!

BRIDE: I am happy. When I said "Yes," it was because I wanted to.

MOTHER: Of course. *(taking her by the chin)* Look at me.

FATHER: She's like my wife—in every way.

MOTHER: Yes? What beautiful eyes! Do you know what being married is, child?

BRIDE: *(gravely)* I know.

MOTHER: One man, some children—and a wall six feet thick to shut out everything else.

BRIDEGROOM: Is anything else needed?

MOTHER: No. Just that you all live. Just that! Live!

BRIDE: I will know my duty.

MOTHER: Here are some presents.

BRIDE: Thank you.

FATHER: Shall we have something?

MOTHER: Nothing for me. *(to* BRIDEGROOM*)* What about you?

BRIDEGROOM: I will. *(He takes a sweet. The* BRIDE *takes one also.)*

FATHER: *(to the* BRIDEGROOM*)* Some wine?

MOTHER: He doesn't touch it.

FATHER: That is best. *(Pause. Everyone is standing.)*

BRIDEGROOM: *(to the* BRIDE*)* I'll come tomorrow.

BRIDE: At what time?

BRIDEGROOM: At five.

BRIDE: I'll be waiting for you.

BRIDEGROOM: When I leave your side, I feel a great separation, and I get a lump in my throat.

BRIDE: When you're my husband, you won't feel that way.

BRIDEGROOM: That's what I say.

MOTHER: We must go. The sun does not wait. *(to the* FATHER*)* Is everything agreed?

FATHER: Agreed.

MOTHER: *(to the* MAID*)* Good-bye.

MAID: Go with God.

(The MOTHER *kisses the* BRIDE, *and they are leaving in silence.)*

MOTHER: *(at the door)* Good-bye, daughter.

(The BRIDE *answers with her hand.)*

FATHER: I will go out with you. *(They leave.)*

MAID: I'm bursting to see the presents!

BRIDE: *(harshly)* Stop it!

MAID: Oh child, show them to me!

BRIDE: I don't want to.

MAID: At least the stockings! They say they're all lace! Please!

BRIDE: I said no!

MAID: For heaven's sake! All right. You're acting like you don't want to get married.

BRIDE: *(biting her hand in rage)* OH!

MAID: Child! My dear! What's the matter with you? Are you sorry you're giving up the life of a queen? Don't think about unpleasant things! Is there any reason? None. Let's look at the presents. *(She takes the box.)*

BRIDE: *(seizing her by the wrists)* Let go!

MAID: Oh, child!

BRIDE: Let go, I said!

MAID: You're stronger than a man!

BRIDE: Haven't I done the work of a man? If only I *were* a man!

MAID: Don't talk like that!

BRIDE: Be quiet, I said! Let's talk about something else.

(The light begins to fade. A long pause.)

MAID: Did you hear a horse last night?

BRIDE: At what time?

MAID: At three o'clock.

BRIDE: It must have been a horse that strayed from the herd.

MAID: No, it had a rider.

BRIDE: How do you know that?

MAID: Because I saw him. He was standing under your window. It really bothered me.

BRIDE: Could it have been my fiancé? Sometimes he comes by at that hour.

MAID: No.

BRIDE: Did you see him?

MAID: Yes.

BRIDE: Who was it?

MAID: It was Leonardo.

BRIDE: *(loudly)* That's a lie! A lie! What would he come here for?

MAID: He came.

BRIDE: Shut up! Damn your tongue!

(The sound of hoofbeats is heard.)

MAID: *(at the window)* Look—out there! Was it him?
BRIDE: It was him.

FAST CURTAIN

END OF ACT I

ACT II

ᢙᢙᢙ

SCENE 1

The veranda of the BRIDE'*s house. The front door is in the background. It is night. The* BRIDE *comes out, dressed in ruffled white petticoats covered with lace and embroidered scallops, a white bodice, and with bare arms. The* MAID *is dressed as she was before.*

MAID: I'll finish combing your hair out here.
BRIDE: It's impossible to stay indoors in this heat!
MAID: It never cools off around here, not even at dawn!

(The BRIDE *sits and looks at herself in a small hand mirror. The* MAID *combs her hair.)*

BRIDE: My mother came from a place where there were many trees, from a fertile land.
MAID: That's why she was so cheerful.
BRIDE: But she wasted away here.
MAID: Fate.
BRIDE: Just as we women all waste away. The walls are throwing off heat! Ouch! Don't pull so much!
MAID: I just want to do this wave better. I want it to fall over your forehead. *(The* BRIDE *looks at herself in the mirror.)* How beautiful you are! Oh! *(She kisses her with great affection.)*

26

BRIDE: *(severely)* Keep combing my hair.

MAID: *(combing)* You are so lucky! You are going to hold a man in your arms. You are going to kiss him. You are going to feel his weight!

BRIDE: Be quiet!

MAID: And the best part is when you wake up and you feel him beside you—and his breath caresses your shoulder like a nightingale's feather!

BRIDE: *(fiercely)* Will you be quiet!

MAID: But child! A wedding—what is it? A wedding is that, and nothing more! Is it the wedding cake? Is it the bouquets of flowers? No! It's a shining bed! And a man! And a woman!

BRIDE: You're not supposed to talk about it!

MAID: That's something else. But it's such fun!

BRIDE: Or such misery!

MAID: I am going to set the orange blossoms from here to here so they form a crown that stands out on top of your hairdo. *(She tries on the orange blossoms.)*

BRIDE: *(looking in the mirror)* Give it to me. *(She takes the orange blossoms, looks at them, and hangs her head dejectedly.)*

MAID: What is this?

BRIDE: Leave me alone.

MAID: This is no time to be sad. *(with spirit)* Give me those flowers! *(The BRIDE throws down the flowers.)* Child, you're asking for trouble, throwing your crown on the floor! Lift up that head. Don't you want to get married? Say so. You can still change your mind.

BRIDE: They're dark clouds—an ill wind inside me. Who hasn't felt that?

MAID: Do you love him?

BRIDE: I love him.

MAID: Yes, yes. I'm sure.

BRIDE: But this is a very big step.

MAID: You have to take it.

BRIDE: I have already given my promise.

MAID: I am going to put the crown on you.

BRIDE: Hurry! They should be arriving soon.
MAID: They've already been on the road at least two hours.
BRIDE: How far is it from here to the church?
MAID: Five leagues by way of the river, but it's twice as far along
    the road.

(The BRIDE *stands; the* MAID *gazes at her with excitement.)*

> The bride is awaking
> On the morning of the wedding!
> Let the rivers of the world
> Carry your crown!

BRIDE: *(smiling)* Come on!
MAID: *(kisses* BRIDE *enthusiastically and dances around her)*

> May she awaken
> With the tender blossom
> Of the laurel in flower!

> May she awaken
> By the trunk and the tendril
> Of the laurel in flower!

(There is a loud knocking.)

BRIDE: Open it! It must be the first guests!

(The BRIDE *goes into the house. The* MAID *opens the door.)*

MAID: *(surprised)* You?
LEONARDO: Me. Good morning.
MAID: You're the first one.
LEONARDO: Wasn't I invited?
MAID: Yes.
LEONARDO: That's why I came.
MAID: Where's your wife?

LEONARDO: I rode the horse. She's coming along the road.
MAID: Didn't you come across anyone?
LEONARDO: I passed them on the horse.
MAID: You're going to kill that animal with so much hard riding!
LEONARDO: When he dies, he's dead.

(Pause.)

MAID: Sit down. Nobody's up yet.
LEONARDO: What about the bride?
MAID: I am going to dress her right now.
LEONARDO: The bride! She must be happy.
MAID: *(changing the subject)* Where is the child?
LEONARDO: What child?
MAID: Your son.
LEONARDO: *(as if from a daze)* Oh.
MAID: Are they bringing him?
LEONARDO: No.

(There is a pause. In the distance, VOICES are singing.)

VOICES:
    The bride is awaking
    On the morning of the wedding!
LEONARDO:
    The bride is awaking
    On the morning of the wedding!
MAID: It's our people. They are still a way off.
LEONARDO: *(rising)* The bride will wear a large crown, won't she?
    It shouldn't be too large. A smaller one would suit her better.
    Did the groom bring the orange blossom she's to wear on her
    breast?

(The BRIDE enters, still in petticoats, wearing the crown of blossoms.)

BRIDE: He brought it.

MAID: Don't come out here like that!

BRIDE: What does it matter? *(coldly)* Why do you ask if they brought the orange blossom? Do you have something in mind?

LEONARDO: Nothing. What would I have in mind? *(approaching her)* You, who know me—you know I don't. Tell me, what have I ever been to you? Open and refresh your memory! Two oxen and a broken-down hut are almost nothing. That's what hurts.

BRIDE: Why did you come?

LEONARDO: To see your wedding.

BRIDE: Just as I saw yours!

LEONARDO: You tied the knot with your own two hands. You can kill me, but you can't spit on me! And gold may glisten—but sometimes it spits!

BRIDE: That's a lie!

LEONARDO: I don't want to talk about it because I'm hot-blooded, and I don't want all these hills to hear my shouts.

BRIDE: My shouts would be louder!

MAID: This conversation cannot continue! You must not talk about the past. *(She glances uneasily at the doors.)*

BRIDE: She's right. I shouldn't even be talking to you. But it makes me furious to have you come and watch me, and pry into my wedding, and make insinuations about the orange blossom. Get out! And wait for your wife at the door!

LEONARDO: You mean you and I can't talk?

MAID: *(furious)* No! You can't talk!

LEONARDO: Since my wedding, I've thought night and day about who was guilty. And every time I think about it, there is a new guilt that swallows up the old. But there is always guilt.

BRIDE: A man on his horse knows the world, and he has the power to squeeze the life out of a lonely girl stranded in a desert. But I have pride—that's why I'm getting married! And I will close myself up with my husband whom I must love more than anything!

LEONARDO: Pride won't do you any good. *(He comes closer.)*

BRIDE: Don't come near me!

LEONARDO: To keep still when you're on fire is the worst punishment we can inflict on ourselves. What good did it do me to have pride? —And not see you? —And leave you lying awake night after night? No good at all! It only poured fire over me! Because you may believe that time can heal and walls can hide—but it's not true. It's not true! When things reach deep inside you, nothing can pull them out!

BRIDE: (trembling) I can't listen to you! I can't listen to your voice! It's as if I drank a bottle of anisette and fell asleep on a blanket of roses. And it draws me under, and I know I'm drowning, but I follow.

MAID: (seizing LEONARDO by the lapels) You must leave here right now!

LEONARDO: It's the last time I'll ever talk to her. Don't worry about a thing.

BRIDE: And I know I'm crazy, and I know I'm rotting away inside with the suffering, and here I am—quietly listening to him, watching him move his arms!

LEONARDO: I can't have peace if I don't tell you these things. I got married. Now you get married!

MAID: She is getting married!

VOICES: (nearer now)
    The bride is awaking
    On the morning of the wedding!

BRIDE: The bride is awaking! (She exits, running to her room.)

MAID: The people are here now. (to LEONARDO) Don't come near her again!

LEONARDO: Don't worry. (He exits, stage left.)

(It begins to grow lighter.)

FIRST GIRL: (entering)
    The bride is awaking

On the morning of the wedding!
The circle turns, and brings a crown
To every balcony.

VOICES:
The bride is awaking!

MAID: *(inspiring their enthusiastic cheers)*
Let her awaken
With the tender blossom,
Of the laurel in flower.

Let her awaken
By the trunk and the tendril
Of the laurel in flower.

SECOND GIRL: *(entering)*
Let her awaken
With her long hair flowing,
A nightgown of snowflakes,
Silver leather slippers,
And jasmine on her forehead.

MAID:
O Shepherdess,
The moon is rising!

FIRST GIRL:
O gallant lover,
Leave your hat in the orchard!

FIRST YOUNG MAN: *(enters with his hat held high)*
The bride is awaking.
The guests are arriving
To dance at her wedding,
With garlands of dahlias,
And cakes for the wedding.

VOICES:
The bride is awaking!

SECOND GIRL:
The bride is now wearing
Her white bridal crown.

The bridegroom has pinned it
With ribbons of gold.
MAID:
Under the citrus tree
The bride awake will be.
THIRD GIRL:
Under the orange bloom,
His tablecloth, his spoon.

(*Three* GUESTS enter.)

FIRST YOUNG MAN:
Awaken, my dove!
The white dawn is shaking
Bells in the shade.
GUEST:
The bride, the white bride—
Today, a maiden;
Tomorrow, a woman.
FIRST GIRL:
Come down, dusky maiden,
Trailing your train made of silk.
WEDDING GUEST:
Come down, dusky maiden,
Fresh with the cool morning dew.
FIRST YOUNG MAN:
Awaken, Señora, awaken!
There are blossoms of orange on the breeze.
MAID:
I want to embroider a tree
Covered with garnet ribbons,
With words of love on each ribbon,
And shouts of praise all around!
VOICES:
The bride is awaking!

FIRST YOUNG MAN:
   On the morning of the wedding!
GUEST:
   On the morning of the wedding,
   How enchanting you will be—
   Like a flower of the mountains!
   Like the wife of a captain!
FATHER: (entering)
   The wife of a captain
   Is taking the bridegroom!
   He comes with his oxen
   To capture the treasure!
THIRD GIRL:
   The bridegroom is golden—
   A golden flower.
   Wherever he travels,
   There are flowers in his footsteps.
MAID:
   O my happy child!
SECOND YOUNG MAN:
   The bride is awaking!
MAID:
   O my enchantress!
FIRST GIRL:
   The wedding guests are calling
   Underneath your window.
SECOND GIRL:
   The bride will come out now!
FIRST GIRL:
   Come out now! Come out now!
MAID:
   They're ringing!
   Bells are ringing!
FIRST YOUNG MAN:
   She's coming here!
   She's coming now!

MAID:
  The excitement is rising
  Like a bull in the ring!

(The BRIDE *appears. She wears a turn-of-the-century black dress, with flowers at the hip, a long train covered with pleated gauze and heavy lace, with the orange-blossom wreath in her hair. Guitars play. The* GIRLS *kiss the* BRIDE.)

THIRD GIRL: What perfume did you put in your hair?
BRIDE: *(laughing)* None!
SECOND GIRL: *(looking at her dress)* You won't find material like
  this anywhere!
FIRST YOUNG MAN: Here's the groom!
BRIDEGROOM: Greetings!
FIRST GIRL: *(putting a flower behind his ear)*
  The groom is gold—
  A golden flower.
SECOND GIRL:
  A peaceful light
  Shines from his eyes.

(The BRIDEGROOM *goes to the* BRIDE's *side.)*

BRIDE: Why did you wear those shoes?
BRIDEGROOM: They're more cheerful than the black ones.

*(*LEONARDO's WIFE *enters and kisses the* BRIDE.)

WIFE: Best wishes!

(The CROWD *is chattering loudly.)*

LEONARDO: *(entering as if to fulfill a duty)*
  On the morning of your marriage
  We are crowning you with flowers.

WIFE:
> So the meadows may be merry
> With the fragrance of your hair.

MOTHER: *(to* FATHER*)* Are those people here too?

FATHER: They are family. Today is a day for forgiveness.

MOTHER: I'll put up with them, but I won't forgive them!

BRIDEGROOM: It makes me happy to see you in your crown!

BRIDE: Let's leave for the church soon.

BRIDEGROOM: Are you in a hurry?

BRIDE: Yes. I am longing to be your wife. And to be alone with you and hear no other voice but yours.

BRIDEGROOM: That's what I want.

BRIDE: And see no other eyes but yours. And have you hold me so tight that even if my dead mother called to me, I couldn't pull myself away from you.

BRIDEGROOM: My arms are strong. I am going to hold you for the next forty years.

BRIDE: *(dramatically, taking him by the arm)* Always!

FATHER: Let's go right away! Get the horses and the carts! The sun has already come up!

MOTHER: But be careful. Let's not have anything go wrong.

(The large door upstage opens, and they begin to exit.)

MAID: *(weeping)*
> On leaving your house,
> Maiden so pure,
> Remember: you leave
> Like a star!

FIRST GIRL:
> Pure in your body and spirit,
> On leaving your house for the wedding!

SECOND GIRL: *(as they leave)*
> You're leaving your home
> To go to the church.

MAID:
> The breeze is tossing flowers
> Along the sands.

THIRD GIRL:
> Oh, the girl is pure!

MAID:
> The lace of her mantilla
> Is like a shady breeze.

(They exit. We hear the music of guitars, sticks, and tambourines.
LEONARDO *and his* WIFE *are left alone on the stage.)*

WIFE: Let's go.

LEONARDO: Where?

WIFE: To the church. But you're not going on your horse, you're coming with me.

LEONARDO: In the cart?

WIFE: What other way?

LEONARDO: I am not a man who rides in a cart!

WIFE: And I am not a woman who goes to a wedding without her husband. I can't stand it any more!

LEONARDO: Neither can I.

WIFE: Why do you look at me like that? There's a dagger in each eye!

LEONARDO: Let's go!

WIFE: I don't know what's happening. But I imagine things, and I don't want to. One thing I know: I've already been tossed aside! But I have a son. And another on the way. Let's get going. My mother had the same fate. But I'm not moving from here!

*(*VOICES *are heard outside.)*

VOICES:
> On leaving your house
> To go to the church,

Remember: you leave
Like a star!
WIFE: *(weeping)*
Remember: you leave
Like a star!

That's how I left my house, too! I could taste the whole world
in my mouth!
LEONARDO: *(rising)* Let's go!
WIFE: But with me!
LEONARDO: Yes. *(pause)* Get going!

(They exit.)

VOICES:
On leaving your house
To go to the church,
Remember: you leave
Like a star!

SLOW CURTAIN

ACT II

⚘⚘⚘

SCENE 2

The exterior of the BRIDE'*s cave. Shades of whites, greys, and cool blues. Large fig trees. Somber, silvered tones. Views of tablelands the color of paste, and everything as hard as a landscape on an inexpensive ceramic piece. The* MAID *is arranging glasses and trays on a table.*

MAID:
Turning—
The wheel was turning,
And the water was flowing.
The wedding approaches!
Let the branches spread open
And the moon embellish
Her white veranda!

(loudly)
Spread the tablecloths!

(with pathos)
Singing—
The lovers were singing,
And the water was flowing.

The wedding approaches!
Let the frost shine and sparkle!
Let the bitter almonds
Be filled with honey!

(loudly)
Bring out the wine!

(poetically)
My lady—
My lady of the land,
See the water flowing!
Your wedding approaches!
You must gather your trousseau
Under the wing of your bridegroom.
Never go from your house—
Because your bridegroom's a dove,
With his whole heart, an ember!

The fields await the murmur
Of the blood that has been spilled.
Turning—
The wheel was turning,
And the water was flowing.
Your wedding approaches!
Let the shining water be glowing!

MOTHER: *(entering)* At last!

FATHER: Are we the first?

MAID: No. Leonardo arrived with his wife a while ago. They must
have driven like demons! His wife arrived frightened to death.
They got here as quickly as if they had come on horseback.

FATHER: That man looks for trouble. He has bad blood.

MOTHER: What blood would he have? That of his whole family,
beginning with his great-grandfather who started the killing,
and on through the whole evil clan! Men who use knives! People with false smiles!

FATHER: Let's leave it alone!

MAID: How can she leave it alone?

MOTHER: I ache down to the end of my veins! On all their faces, I see nothing but the hand that killed what was mine. Do you see me? Don't I seem mad to you? Well, I am mad—from not having shouted everything I needed to. I have a scream in my throat—always there—that I have to choke back and hide under my shawl. But they carry off the dead and you must keep silent. Or people will criticize. (*She takes off her shawl.*)

FATHER: Today is not the day for you to remember these things.

MOTHER: When it comes up in conversation, I have to speak. And today more than ever, because today I'm left alone in my house.

FATHER: In hopes of having new company.

MOTHER: That's my dream. Grandchildren.

(*They sit down.*)

FATHER: I want them to have many. This land needs hands that are not hired. We have to keep up a battle—with weeds, thistles, and rocks that come from who knows where. And these hands should belong to the owners—hands that will punish and will dominate and will sow the seeds. Many sons are needed.

MOTHER: And some daughters! Boys are like the wind. They are forced to use weapons. Girls never leave the house.

FATHER: (*cheerfully*) I think they'll have everything!

MOTHER: My son will do well by her. He comes from good stock. His father could have had many sons with me.

FATHER: What I would like is for it all to happen in one day! For them to have two or three grown sons right away!

MOTHER: But it's not like that. It takes so much time. That's why it's so terrible to see your own blood spilled on the ground. A fountain that flows for a minute—and takes years out of our lives! When I got to see my son, he was lying in the middle of the street. My hands were wet with blood, and I licked them with my tongue. Because it was mine! You don't know what that is! In an urn of crystal and topaz, I would place the earth soaked with his blood!

FATHER: Now you must wait. My daughter is healthy and your son is strong.

MOTHER: I hope so.

(They stand up.)

FATHER: Prepare the trays of wheat!

MAID: They are ready.

WIFE: *(entering)* I hope all is well!

MOTHER: Thank you.

LEONARDO: Will there be a fiesta?

FATHER: A little one. People can't stay too late.

MAID: They have arrived!

(GUESTS *begin entering in lively groups. The* BRIDE *and* BRIDE-GROOM *enter, arm in arm.* LEONARDO *exits.)*

BRIDEGROOM: I've never seen so many people at a wedding!

BRIDE: *(gloomily)* Never.

FATHER: It was magnificent!

MOTHER: Entire branches of families have come!

BRIDEGROOM: People who never used to leave their houses!

MOTHER: Your father sowed many seeds, and now you reap them.

BRIDEGROOM: There were cousins of mine that I didn't know any more!

MOTHER: All the people from the coast.

BRIDEGROOM: *(laughing)* They were amazed at the horses!

(Everyone is talking.)

MOTHER: *(to the* BRIDE*)* What are you thinking about?

BRIDE: I'm not thinking about anything.

MOTHER: The wedding vows weigh heavily.

(Guitars are playing.)

BRIDE: Like lead!
MOTHER: *(strongly)* But they shouldn't! You should feel as light as a dove.
BRIDE: Are you staying here tonight?
MOTHER: No. There is no one at my house.
BRIDE: You should stay!
FATHER: *(to* MOTHER) Look at the dance they have started! Dances from way over there by the edge of the sea.

(LEONARDO enters and sits down. His WIFE stands behind him, stiffly.)

MOTHER: They are my husband's cousins. As hard as rocks when they dance.
FATHER: I enjoy watching them. What a change for this house! *(He exits.)*
BRIDEGROOM: *(to* BRIDE) Did you like the orange blossom?
BRIDE: *(staring at him)* Yes.
BRIDEGROOM: It's all made of wax. It lasts forever. I would have liked you to wear them all over your dress.
BRIDE: There's no need.

(LEONARDO exits right.)

FIRST GIRL: Let's go and take off your pins.
BRIDE: *(to* BRIDEGROOM) I'll be right back. *(BRIDE and* FIRST GIRL *exit.)*
WIFE: I hope you will be happy with my cousin!
BRIDEGROOM: I'm sure I will be.
WIFE: The two of you here, without ever leaving, raising a family. How I wish I, too, could live this far away!
BRIDEGROOM: Why don't you buy some land? It's cheap on the hillside and better for raising children.
WIFE: We don't have any money. And the way things are going . . .

BRIDEGROOM: Your husband is a hard worker.

WIFE: Yes. But he likes to keep moving a lot. He goes from one thing to another. He's not a man who has settled down.

MAID: Aren't you eating anything? I am going to wrap up some wine biscuits for your mother—she likes them so much.

BRIDEGROOM: Give her three dozen.

WIFE: No, no! Half a dozen will be enough.

BRIDEGROOM: This is a special day.

WIFE: *(to* MAID) Where is Leonardo?

MAID: I didn't see him.

BRIDEGROOM: He must be with the others.

WIFE: I will go and see! *(She leaves.)*

MAID: That is beautiful!

BRIDEGROOM: You're not dancing?

MAID: No one asked me.

(TWO GIRLS cross upstage. During this entire scene, people cross upstage animatedly.)

BRIDEGROOM: *(cheerfully)* That's because they don't know any better. Lively old ladies like you dance better than young ones.

MAID: Are you trying to flatter me, young man? That family of yours! Men among men! When I was a child, I went to your grandfather's wedding. What stature! It was as if a mountain was getting married!

BRIDEGROOM: I am not as tall.

MAID: But you have the same gleam in your eyes. Where's the child?

BRIDEGROOM: Taking off her crown.

MAID: Ah! Look, for midnight, since you won't be asleep, I prepared some ham and some large glasses of old wine. In the lower part of the cupboard. In case you need it.

BRIDEGROOM: *(smiling)* I don't eat at midnight.

MAID: If not you, the bride. *(She exits.)*

FIRST YOUTH: *(entering)* You have to drink with us!

BRIDEGROOM: I am waiting for the bride.

SECOND YOUTH: Her, you'll have at daybreak!
FIRST YOUTH: That's when it's the most fun!
SECOND YOUTH: Just for a minute!
BRIDEGROOM: Let's go.

(*They exit. There is loud cheering. The* BRIDE *enters. The* TWO
GIRLS *run to meet her from the opposite side of the stage.*)

FIRST GIRL: Who did you give the first pin to, to me or to this one?
BRIDE: I don't remember.
FIRST GIRL: You gave it to me, here!
SECOND GIRL: To me, in front of the altar!
BRIDE: (*restless, in an inner struggle*) I don't know anything.
FIRST GIRL: I just wish that you'd—
BRIDE: (*interrupting*) And I don't care! I have a lot to think about.
SECOND GIRL: Excuse me.

(LEONARDO *crosses upstage.*)

BRIDE: (*seeing* LEONARDO) And these are anxious moments.
FIRST GIRL: We don't know anything!
BRIDE: You will know when your time comes. This step is one that
    costs you dearly.
FIRST GIRL: Are you upset with us?
BRIDE: No. Please forgive me.
SECOND GIRL: For what? But both pins mean you get married,
    don't they?
BRIDE: Both.
FIRST GIRL: But one of us will get married before the other.
BRIDE: Do you want it so badly?
SECOND GIRL: (*shyly*) Yes.
BRIDE: Why?
FIRST GIRL: Well . . .

(FIRST GIRL *embraces the other. They both run off. The* BRIDE-
GROOM *enters very slowly and embraces the* BRIDE *from behind.*)

BRIDE: *(in sudden fear)* Get away!

BRIDEGROOM: Do I frighten you?

BRIDE: Oh! It was you?

BRIDEGROOM: Who would it be? *(pause)* Your father or me.

BRIDE: That's true.

BRIDEGROOM: But your father would have embraced you more gently.

BRIDE: *(gloomily)* Of course.

(The BRIDEGROOM embraces her fiercely, in a way that is a bit brusque.)

BRIDEGROOM: Because he is old!

BRIDE: *(dryly)* Let me go.

BRIDEGROOM: Why? *(He lets her go.)*

BRIDE: Because . . . people . . . They can see us!

(The MAID crosses upstage again, without looking at the couple.)

BRIDEGROOM: What of it? It is blessed now!

BRIDE: Yes, but let me go. Later.

BRIDEGROOM: What is wrong? You seem to be frightened.

BRIDE: Nothing is wrong. Don't go.

(LEONARDO's WIFE enters.)

WIFE: I don't want to interrupt . . .

BRIDEGROOM: What is it?

WIFE: Did my husband come through here?

BRIDE: No.

WIFE: You see, I can't find him. And his horse isn't in the stable either.

BRIDEGROOM: *(cheerfully)* He must be out riding.

(The WIFE exits, uneasily. The MAID enters.)

MAID: Aren't you happy about so many good wishes?

BRIDEGROOM: I wish it were already over. The bride is a little tired.

MAID: What is it, child?

BRIDE: There's a sort of pounding in my temples.

MAID: In these hills, a bride must be strong. (to the BRIDE-GROOM) You're the only one who can cure her, because she belongs to you. (The MAID goes off quickly.)

BRIDEGROOM: (embracing her) Let's join the dancing for a while. (He kisses her.)

BRIDE: (in anguish) No. I want to lie down a while.

BRIDEGROOM: I'll keep you company.

BRIDE: Never! With all these people here? What would they say? Let me rest a moment.

BRIDEGROOM: Whatever you like. But don't be like this tonight!

BRIDE: (at the door) By tonight I will be better.

BRIDEGROOM: Which is what I want!

(The MOTHER enters.)

MOTHER: Son.

BRIDEGROOM: Where have you been?

MOTHER: In all that noise. Are you happy?

BRIDEGROOM: Yes.

MOTHER: Where is your wife?

BRIDEGROOM: She's resting a little. It's a bad day for brides.

MOTHER: A bad day? It's the only good one! For me, it was like an inheritance! (The MAID enters and goes toward the BRIDE's room.) It's the plowing of land, the planting of new trees.

BRIDEGROOM: Are you going to leave?

MOTHER: Yes. I have to be at my house.

BRIDEGROOM: Alone.

MOTHER: Not alone. My head is full of things—and of men and struggles.

BRIDEGROOM: But struggles that are no longer struggles.

(The MAID enters quickly. She exits, running, upstage.)

MOTHER: While you live, you struggle.

BRIDEGROOM: I always respect your wishes.

MOTHER: With your wife, try to be affectionate. And if you notice her being distant or shy, caress her in a way that will hurt her a bit. A strong embrace, a little bite—and then a soft kiss. Not enough to upset her, but enough for her to know you are the man, the master, the one who gives the orders. That's how I learned from your father. And since you don't have him, I must be the one to teach you these strategies.

BRIDEGROOM: I will always do what you say.

FATHER: (*entering*) Where is my daughter?

BRIDEGROOM: She's inside.

FIRST GIRL: Come on, bride and groom! We're going to dance the Wheel!

FIRST YOUTH: (*to* BRIDEGROOM) You're going to lead it.

FATHER: (*as he comes out*) She's not here!

BRIDEGROOM: No?

FATHER: She must have gone out on the balcony.

BRIDEGROOM: I'm going to see! (*He exits; crowd noises and guitars are heard.*)

FIRST GIRL: They've already started! (*She exits.*)

BRIDEGROOM: (*entering*) She's not there.

MOTHER: (*uneasily*) No?

FATHER: Where could she have gone?

MAID: (*entering*) The child, where is she?

MOTHER: (*gravely*) We don't know.

(*The* BRIDEGROOM *exits. Three* GUESTS *enter.*)

FATHER: (*dramatically*) But isn't she in the dance?

MAID: She's not in the dance.

FATHER: (*shocked*) There are so many people. Go look!

MAID: I've already looked!

FATHER: (*tragically*) Well, where is she?

BRIDEGROOM: (*entering*) Nothing. She's not anywhere.

MOTHER: (*to* FATHER) What is this? Where is your daughter?

(LEONARDO's WIFE *enters.*)

WIFE: They ran away! They ran away! She and Leonardo! On the horse! They rode off in each other's arms, like a bolt of lightning!

FATHER: It's not true! My daughter? No!

MOTHER: Your daughter, yes! Born of an evil mother, and him— him, too! But now she is my son's wife!

BRIDEGROOM: Let's go after them! Who has a horse?

MOTHER: Who has a horse? Right now—who has a horse? I'll give you everything I have: my eyes and even my tongue!

VOICE: There's one here!

MOTHER: *(to* BRIDEGROOM*)* Go! After them! *(He leaves with two* YOUNG MEN.*)* No! Don't go! Those people kill quickly and well! But—yes: run! And I'll follow.

FATHER: It can't be her! Perhaps she has thrown herself into the cistern!

MOTHER: Honorable women throw themselves into the water, the decent ones. Not that one! But now she's my son's wife! *(Everyone enters.)* Two sides! There are two sides here! My family and yours! Everyone, leave here! Clean the dust from your shoes! We are going to help my son!

(The CROWD *separates into two groups.)*

Because he has his people—his cousins from the sea! And all those who came from the interior! Out of here! Along every road! It has come once again—the hour of blood! Two sides! You with yours and me with mine! After them! After them!

CURTAIN

END OF ACT II

ACT III

∽∽∽

SCENE 1

A forest at night with great moist tree trunks and a murky atmosphere. Two violins are playing.

FIRST WOODCUTTER: And have they found them?

SECOND WOODCUTTER: No. But they're searching everywhere.

THIRD WOODCUTTER: They will find them soon.

SECOND WOODCUTTER: Shhh!

THIRD WOODCUTTER: What?

SECOND WOODCUTTER: They seem to be closing in on every road at once.

FIRST WOODCUTTER: When the moon comes out, they will see them.

SECOND WOODCUTTER: They should leave them alone. The world is wide—everyone can live in it.

FIRST WOODCUTTER: But they will kill them.

SECOND WOODCUTTER: You must follow your heart. They did well to run away.

FIRST WOODCUTTER: They had been lying to each other. But in the end, blood was stronger!

THIRD WOODCUTTER: Blood!

FIRST WOODCUTTER: You must follow the course of your blood.

50

SECOND WOODCUTTER: But blood that is spilled is soaked up by the earth.

FIRST WOODCUTTER: What of it? Better to be a corpse without blood than to be alive with it festering.

THIRD WOODCUTTER: Be quiet!

FIRST WOODCUTTER: What? Do you hear something?

THIRD WOODCUTTER: I hear the crickets, the frogs, the ambush of the night.

FIRST WOODCUTTER: But you don't hear the horse.

THIRD WOODCUTTER: No.

FIRST WOODCUTTER: Now he must be making love to her.

SECOND WOODCUTTER: Her body was meant for him and his body for her.

THIRD WOODCUTTER: They will track them down and kill them.

FIRST WOODCUTTER: But their blood will have mingled by then! They will be like two empty water jars, like two dry rivers.

SECOND WOODCUTTER: There are many clouds, and it will be easy for the moon not to come out.

THIRD WOODCUTTER: The bridegroom will find them—with the moon or without the moon! I saw him start off—like a raging star! His face, the color of ashes, expressed the fate of his whole family.

FIRST WOODCUTTER: His family of corpses in the middle of the street!

SECOND WOODCUTTER: That's right.

THIRD WOODCUTTER: Do you think they will manage to break through the circle?

SECOND WOODCUTTER: It would be difficult. There are knives and guns for ten leagues around.

THIRD WOODCUTTER: He's riding a good horse . . .

SECOND WOODCUTTER: But he is carrying a woman with him!

FIRST WOODCUTTER: We are close now.

SECOND WOODCUTTER: A tree with forty branches. We'll soon cut it down.

THIRD WOODCUTTER: The moon is coming out now. Let's hurry!

(The lights grow brighter at stage left.)

FIRST WOODCUTTER:
   O rising moon!
   Moon of the giant leaves.
SECOND WOODCUTTER:
   The blood is filled with jasmine!
FIRST WOODCUTTER:
   O lonely moon!
   Moon of the tender leaves.
SECOND WOODCUTTER:
   Silver on the face of the bride!
THIRD WOODCUTTER:
   O evil moon!
   Leave the dark bough for their love!
FIRST WOODCUTTER:
   O somber moon!
   Leave the dark bough for their love!

(They exit. The MOON *appears in the light at stage left. The* MOON *is a young woodcutter with a white face. The stage takes on a vivid blue brilliance.)*

MOON:
   I'm a round swan on the river.
   I'm the cathedrals' eye.
   I'm the false dawn in the treetops.
   They will not get away!
   Who's hiding there? Who sobs
   Beneath the thorns and brambles?
   The moon drops down a dagger,
   Abandoned in the air—
   A plumb of lead that wants to be
   The agony of blood.
   Let me in! I come, frozen,

Through the walls and windows;
Open your roofs, your flesh,
Where I can warm myself!
I am cold! My ashes
Of heavy, sleeping metals
Seek the crest of the fire
Through streets and mountains.

But the snow will carry me
Upon its jasper shoulder.
I'll sink beneath the water
Of the frozen ponds.
And so tonight I'll have
Red blood for my cheeks
And the reeds that huddle
At the wide feet of the wind.
There'll be no shade, no shadow—
They will not get away!
I want to enter a breast
So I can warm myself!
A heart! A heart for me—
Feverish, let it flow
Over the hills of my breast.
Let me in! Oh, let me!

(to the boughs)
I want no shadows. My rays
Must enter everywhere:
Among the darkened trees,
A murmuring of light.
So that tonight I'll have
Sweet blood upon my cheeks
And the reeds that huddle
At the wide feet of the wind.
Who is hiding? Come out, I say!
No! They can not escape!

I will make the horse shine bright
With a feverish diamond light!

(*The* MOON *disappears between the tree trunks, and the stage
lights dim again. A very old* BEGGAR WOMAN *enters, completely
covered in flimsy, dark-green garments. She is barefoot. Her face
can barely be seen under the folds of cloth. The character does not
appear on the cast list.*)

BEGGAR WOMAN:
    That moon is gone, and they draw near.
    They won't get past. The river's whisper
    And the whispering trunks of trees, will drown
    Their screams, their lacerated screams.
    Here it will be, and soon. I am so tired!
    The coffins open, and clean white sheets
    Are waiting upon the bedroom floor
    For bodies of men whose throats have been torn.
    Let no bird awaken. And let the breeze—
    Gathering their moans in the folds of her skirt—
    Fly with them over the black treetops,
    Or bury them deep in the softness of mud.

(*impatiently*)
    That moon, that moon!

(*The* MOON *appears. The intense blue light returns.*)

MOON:
                                    Now they are near!
    Some through the valley and the other one along the river.
    I'll shine on the rocks. What do you need?
BEGGAR WOMAN:
                                                Nothing.
MOON:
    The wind blows hard, with a double edge.

BEGGAR WOMAN:
Shine on his vest, and open the buttons—
Then later the daggers will follow the way.
MOON:
Let them be a long time dying.
Let blood hiss delicately through my fingers.
See how my ashen valleys waken,
And eagerly await this trembling fountain!
BEGGAR WOMAN:
We won't let them cross the river. Silence!
MOON:
There they come!

(The MOON *exits. The stage lights dim.)*

BEGGAR WOMAN:
                                    Hurry! Lots of light!
Did you hear me? They can not escape!

(The BRIDEGROOM *and the* FIRST YOUNG MAN *enter. The* BEG-
GAR WOMAN *sits down and conceals herself in her shawl.)*

BRIDEGROOM: *(entering)* This way.
FIRST YOUNG MAN: You won't find them.
BRIDEGROOM: *(forcefully)* Yes, I will find them!
FIRST YOUNG MAN: I think they've taken another path.
BRIDEGROOM: No. A moment ago, I heard galloping.
FIRST YOUNG MAN: It must have been another horse.
BRIDEGROOM: *(dramatically)* Listen! There is only one horse in
     the world—and it's this one! Do you understand? If you follow
     me, follow me without talking!
FIRST YOUNG MAN: I just wish—
BRIDEGROOM: Be quiet! I am sure I'll find them here! See this
     arm? Well, it is not my arm—it is the arm of my brother and of
     my father and of everyone in my family who is dead! And it has
     so much power that it can pull this tree up by the roots if it

wants! And let's hurry, because I feel the teeth of my whole family digging into me—here! In a way that makes it impossible for me to breathe easily.

BEGGAR WOMAN: *(whining)* Ay!

FIRST YOUNG MAN: Did you hear that?

BRIDEGROOM: Go that way, and circle back.

FIRST YOUNG MAN: This is a hunt.

BRIDEGROOM: The greatest there can be!

(The FIRST YOUNG MAN *exits. The* BRIDEGROOM *goes rapidly toward the left and stumbles upon the* BEGGAR WOMAN: DEATH.*)*

BEGGAR WOMAN: Ay!

BRIDEGROOM: What do you want?

BEGGAR WOMAN: I am cold!

BRIDEGROOM: Which way are you going?

BEGGAR WOMAN: *(still whining, like a beggar)* That way—far away.

BRIDEGROOM: Where are you coming from?

BEGGAR WOMAN: From there. From very far.

BRIDEGROOM: Did you see a man and a woman race by on horseback?

BEGGAR WOMAN: *(enlivened)* Wait! *(looks at him)* Beautiful young man! *(She gets up.)* But much more beautiful if you were asleep!

BRIDEGROOM: Tell me! Answer! Did you see them?

BEGGAR WOMAN: Wait! What very broad shoulders! Why don't you want to be laid out on them instead of walking around on the soles of such small feet?

BRIDEGROOM: *(shaking her)* I asked you if you saw them! Have they passed through here?

BEGGAR WOMAN: *(forcefully)* They have not passed! But they are coming down the hill. Don't you hear?

BRIDEGROOM: No.

BEGGAR WOMAN: You don't know the road?

BRIDEGROOM: I will go, whatever it's like!
BEGGAR WOMAN: I will go with you. I know this land.
BRIDEGROOM: *(impatiently)* Then let's go! Which way?
BEGGAR WOMAN: *(dramatically)* Through there!

(They exit rapidly. Two violins are heard in the distance. They evoke the forest. The WOODCUTTERS *return with their axes on their shoulders. They walk slowly between the trunks of the trees.)*

FIRST WOODCUTTER:
    Death! Death is coming,
    Beneath the giant leaves!
SECOND WOODCUTTER:
    Don't start the flow of blood!
FIRST WOODCUTTER: *(as he exits)*
    Death, lonely death,
    Beneath the withered leaves.
THIRD WOODCUTTER:
    Don't cover the wedding with flowers!
SECOND WOODCUTTER: *(as he exits)*
    Death, mournful death,
    Leave a green branch for love!
THIRD WOODCUTTER: *(as he exits)*
    Death, vicious death,
    Leave a green branch for love.

*(*LEONARDO *and the* BRIDE *enter.)*

LEONARDO:
    Quiet!
BRIDE:
    From here, I'll go alone!
    Leave! I want you to go back!
LEONARDO:
    Quiet, I said!

BRIDE:

With your teeth,
With your hands—however you can—
Take from my neck this metal chain.
Leave me! Let me live forsaken,
There in my house made of earth.
And if you do not want to kill me,
As you would kill the smallest snake,
Then put the barrel of your gun
Into my hands, the hands of a bride!
A song of sorrow—Burning! Burning!—
Rises up inside my head!
My tongue is pierced with glass.

LEONARDO:

We've taken the step, now. Quiet!
Because they follow us closely,
And I must take you with me.

BRIDE:

Then it must be by force!

LEONARDO:

By force! But which of us went first
Back there? Who led me down the stairs?

BRIDE:

I led the way.

LEONARDO:

Who untied the horse?

BRIDE:

I did. I did. It's true!

LEONARDO:

Whose hands
Put spurs upon my boots?

BRIDE:

These hands that are yours. They ache
To dig into your flesh
And open every vein

To hear your murmuring blood.
I love you! I love you! But leave me!
If I were able to kill you,
I'd wrap you in a shroud
Bordered with violets!
A song of sorrow—burning!—
Rises in my head!

LEONARDO:

My tongue is pierced with glass!
Because I wanted to forget,
I put a wall of stone
Between your house and mine.
It's true! Don't you remember?
Seeing you in the distance,
I filled my eyes with sand!
But I would take my horse,
And the horse would go to your door.
The silver pins of your wedding
Were making my blood turn black.
The dream was filling my flesh
With bitter, choking weeds!
Because the blame's not mine!
The blame belongs to the earth,
And to the smell that comes
From your breasts and from your braids.

BRIDE:

I must be mad! I do not want
To share your bed or food,
Yet every minute of the day
I long to be with you.
You pull me, and I go with you,
And then you push me back.
And helplessly I follow you
Like dust blown on the wind.
I've left a good and honest man,

His family, his house,
In the middle of the wedding,
Still wearing my bridal crown!
But you are the one they will punish,
And I don't want that to be.
Leave me alone! Escape!
No one can help you now.

LEONARDO:
The first wild birds of the morning
Are breaking out of the trees.
And now the night is dying
At the edge of the stony field.
Let's find a corner of darkness
Where I will love you always,
For I don't care about people,
Or the poison that they spread.

(He embraces her tightly.)

BRIDE:
And I will lie at your feet—
Guarding what you dream—
Naked, watching the fields
As if I were your dog.
Because I am! I look at you:
Your beauty makes me burn!

LEONARDO:
Fire is fed by fire.
The same small flame destroys
Two stalks of wheat at once.
Let's go! *(He pulls her.)*

BRIDE:
                    Where will you take me?

LEONARDO:
Somewhere they cannot go,

These men who now surround us—
Where I can look at you!

BRIDE:

And show me at the country fairs,
"The Shame of a Decent Woman"?
So everyone can stare at me
With my wedding sheets unfurled
As if they were my banners?

LEONARDO:

I would want to leave you, too,
If I thought like others think!
But wherever you go, I am going.
And you, too. Take one step. Only try!
The moon nails us together.
My loins are fused to your thighs.

(This entire scene is filled with violent sensuality.)

BRIDE:

Listen!

LEONARDO:

They're coming!

BRIDE:

Run!

It's right for me to die
Here, with my feet in the water
And thorns around my head.
And for the leaves to mourn me:
A lost and fallen maiden!

LEONARDO:

Quiet! They're here now!

BRIDE:

Go!

LEONARDO:

Be silent! Don't let them hear us!
You in front. Let's go, I say!

(*The* BRIDE *hesitates.*)

BRIDE:
   We'll both go together!
LEONARDO: (*embracing her*)
                      As you wish!
   If they separate us, it will be
   Because I am dead.
BRIDE:
                  And I am dead!

(*They exit, their arms around each other.*)

(*The* MOON *emerges, very slowly. The stage takes on an intense blue light. The two violins play. Suddenly, their music is cut short by two long, piercing screams. On the second scream, the* BEGGAR WOMAN *appears and stands with her back to the audience. She opens her cloak and remains at center stage, like a great bird with immense wings. The* MOON *stops. The curtain descends on a complete silence.*)

CURTAIN

ACT III

∽∽∽

SCENE 2

*A white house with arches and thick walls. At left and at right,
white stairways. Upstage, a very large arch, and a wall of the same
color. Even the floor is shining white. This unadorned house has
the monumental feeling of a church. There must not be a single
grey, a single shadow—not even one required for perspective.* TWO
GIRLS *dressed in dark blue are unwinding a* madeja—*a skein of
red wool.*

FIRST GIRL:
  Madeja, madeja,
  What will you make?
SECOND GIRL:
  Clothing of jasmine,
  Paper of crystal,
  Born at four,
  Dead at ten.
  The woolen thread
  A chain at your feet.
  A knot that binds
  Bitter laurel.
YOUNG GIRL: *(singing)*
  Did you go to the wedding?

63

FIRST GIRL:
No.

YOUNG GIRL:
Neither did I!
What could have happened
In the budding vineyard?
What could have happened
In the olive grove?
How could it happen
That no one returned?
Did you go to the wedding?

SECOND GIRL:
We've told you: no.

YOUNG GIRL: *(going)*
Neither did I!

SECOND GIRL:
Madeja, madeja,
What will you sing?

FIRST GIRL:
Wounds of wax,
Salve of sorrow.
Sleeping by morning,
Watching by night.

YOUNG GIRL: *(at the door)*
The thread is caught
Upon the flint.
The azure mountains
Allow it to pass.
It runs and runs and runs
And finally arrives
At the stab of the knife,
The last of the bread.

(She exits.)

SECOND GIRL:
   Madeja, madeja,
   What will you say?
FIRST GIRL:
   The lover is silent,
   And crimson, the groom.
   On the mute river bank,
   I saw them laid out.

(She pauses, staring at the madeja.*)*

YOUNG GIRL:
   The thread runs and runs,
   It runs to here.
   Covered with mud,
   I hear them come.
   Lifeless bodies,
   Sheets of ivory.

(She leaves. LEONARDO's WIFE *and* MOTHER-IN-LAW *enter, in anguish.)*

FIRST GIRL:
   Are they coming now?
MOTHER-IN-LAW: *(sourly)*
                     We don't know.
SECOND GIRL:
   What can you tell us about the wedding?
FIRST GIRL:
   Tell me!
MOTHER-IN-LAW: *(dryly)*
              Nothing.
WIFE:
   I want to return, to know everything.

MOTHER-IN-LAW: *(forcefully)*
    You: go to your house!
    Brave and alone in your house.
    You will grow old and you'll weep.
    Always, the door will be closed.
    Never. Living or dead.
    We'll nail down the windows forever.
    Let the rains come, and nights
    Cover the bitter weeds!
WIFE:
    What could have happened!
MOTHER-IN-LAW:
                              No matter.
    Cover your face with a veil.
    Your children are children of yours,
    Nothing else matters to you.
    You must place a cross made of ashes
    On the bed where his pillow has been.

(WIFE *and* MOTHER-IN-LAW *exit.*)

BEGGAR WOMAN: *(at the door)*
    A piece of bread, little girls!
LITTLE GIRL:
    Go away!
BEGGAR WOMAN:
            Why?
LITTLE GIRL:
                Because
    You whine. Go away!
FIRST GIRL:
                        Child!
BEGGAR WOMAN:
    I could have asked you for your eyes!
    A cloud of birds follows me. Want one?

LITTLE GIRL:
  I want to leave!
SECOND GIRL:
                    Don't pay attention!
FIRST GIRL:
  You came along the river road?
BEGGAR WOMAN:
  I came that way.
FIRST GIRL:
                    Can I ask you—?
BEGGAR WOMAN:
  I saw them. They'll soon be here. Two torrents,
  Lie still at last among the boulders.
  Two men at the feet of the horse.
  Dead in the beauty of the night.

(savoring it)
  Dead! Yes, dead!
FIRST GIRL:
                    Quiet, old woman!
BEGGAR WOMAN:
  Their eyes are broken flowers. Their teeth
  Are just two handfuls of frozen snow.
  They both fell dead. The bride returns
  With bloodstains on her skirt and hair.
  Covered with cloaks, the bodies come,
  Come on the shoulders of tall young men.
  That's how it was. Nothing more. It was just.
  Over the golden flower—filthy sand.

(She leaves. The GIRLS *bow their heads, and start to exit, in step
with each other.)*

FIRST GIRL:
  Filthy sand.

SECOND GIRL:
                    Over the golden flower.
LITTLE GIRL:
    Over the golden flower.
    They bring the dead from the river.
    Young and dark, the one.
    Young and dark, the other.
    The nightingale of shadow
    Soars and grieves,
    Over the golden flower!

(*She leaves. The stage is empty. The* MOTHER *enters with a* NEIGHBOR, *who is weeping.*)

MOTHER: Quiet!
NEIGHBOR: I can't.
MOTHER: Quiet, I said! (*at the doorway*) Is there no one here? (*She puts her hands to her forehead.*) My son should be answering me! But my son is now an armful of withered flowers. My son is now a fading voice behind the mountains. (*angrily, to the* NEIGHBOR) Will you be quiet? I want no weeping in this house. Your tears are tears that come only from your eyes, and mine will come when I am alone—from the soles of my feet, from my roots—and they will burn hotter than blood!
NEIGHBOR: Come to my house. Don't stay here.
MOTHER: Here. Here is where I want to be. And at peace. Now everyone is dead. At midnight, I will sleep—I will sleep at last without being terrified of guns or knives. Other mothers will be looking out their windows, lashed with rain, to see the faces of their sons. Not me. I will make from my dream a cold ivory dove, that will carry camelias of frost over the cemetery. But no!—not the cemetery, not the cemetery!—a cradle in the earth, a bed that shelters them and rocks them in the sky.

(A WOMAN *dressed in black enters, goes to the right, and kneels there.*)

MOTHER: *(to the* NEIGHBOR*)* Take your hands from your face. There are terrible days ahead of us. I don't want to see anyone. The earth and me! My tears and me! And these four walls! Oh! Oh! *(She sits down, overcome.)*

NEIGHBOR: Have pity on yourself.

MOTHER: *(pushing her hair back)* I must be calm. Because the neighbors will be coming, and I don't want them to see how poor I am. How poor! A woman without even one son to touch to her lips!

(The BRIDE *enters, without her orange blossom, wearing a black cape.)*

NEIGHBOR: *(looking at the* BRIDE *angrily)* Where are you going?

BRIDE: I'm coming here.

MOTHER: *(to the* NEIGHBOR*)* Who is it?

NEIGHBOR: Don't you recognize her?

MOTHER: That's why I ask who it is. Because I must not recognize her, so I won't dig my teeth into her neck! You vile serpent! *(She moves threateningly toward the* BRIDE, *then stops. To the* NEIGHBOR*)* You see her? She's there, and she's crying, and I—calm—without tearing her eyes out. I don't understand myself. Could it be that I didn't love my son? But what about his honor? Where is his honor? *(She strikes the* BRIDE, *who falls to the floor.)*

NEIGHBOR: My God! *(She tries to separate them.)*

BRIDE: *(to* NEIGHBOR*)* Let her! I have come so she can kill me and I can be buried with them. *(to the* MOTHER*)* But not with your hands—with grappling hooks, with a sickle, and with all your might—until it breaks on my bones. Go ahead! But I want you to know I am pure. I may be mad, but they can bury me without any man ever having seen himself in the whiteness of my breasts!

MOTHER: Be quiet! Be quiet! What do I care about that?

BRIDE: Because I ran away with another man, I ran away! *(anguished)* You would have gone, too! I was a woman consumed

by fire, covered with open sores inside and out, and your son
was a little bit of water from whom I hoped for children, land,
health! But the other one was a dark river filled with branches
that brought close to me the murmur of its rushes and its whis-
tling song. And I would go with your son, who was like a little
boy bringing me cold water, and the other would send hundreds of birds that blocked my way and left frost on the
wounds of this poor, wasted woman, a girl caressed by fire! I
didn't want to! Listen to me! I didn't want to! Your son was
what I wanted, and I have not deceived him. But the arm of
the other dragged me—like the surge of the sea, like the halter
on a mule—and would have dragged me always, always,
always! Even if I were old and all the sons of your son held me
by the hair!

(*Another* NEIGHBOR *enters.*)

MOTHER: It's not her fault. Nor mine! (*sarcastically*) Whose is it,
then? Loose, weak, indecent woman—who throws off her
bridal crown to look for a piece of bed warmed by another
woman!
BRIDE: Stop it! Stop it! Take your revenge on me! Here I am! See
how soft my neck is? It will be easier than picking a dahlia from
your garden. But that, no! Honorable, as honorable as a new-
born child! And strong enough to prove it to you! Light the fire!
We'll put our hands in it—you, for your son; me, for my body!
You'll take yours out first!

(*Another* NEIGHBOR *comes in.*)

MOTHER: What do I care about your honor? What do I care about
your death? What do I care about anything at all? Blessed be
the fields of wheat, because my sons lie under them. Blessed
be the rain, because it wets the faces of the dead. Blessed be
God who lays us down together to rest.

(Another NEIGHBOR *enters.)*

BRIDE: Let me weep with you.
MOTHER: Weep. But at the door.

*(*LITTLE GIRL *enters. The* BRIDE *remains at the door, the* MOTHER *at the center of the stage.)*

WIFE: *(enters, goes to the left)*
    He was a handsome horseman
    And now he's a bank of snow.
    He rode through the fairs and mountains
    And into the arms of love.
    And now, the moss of night
    Is a crown around his forehead.
MOTHER:
    My child, my son, my sunflower,
    Mirror of the earth:
    Upon your chest, a cross
    Of bitter oleander—
    A sheet to cover you,
    Of shining, silken strands.
    And water forms a sob
    Between your quiet hands.
WIFE:
    Oh, the four young men
    Who come with weary shoulders!
BRIDE:
    Oh, the fair young men
    Who carry death through the air!
MOTHER:
    Neighbors!
LITTLE GIRL: *(at the doorway)*
        They bring them now.

MOTHER:
   It's the same—
   The Cross! The Cross!
WOMEN:
   Sweet nails,
   Sweet Cross,
   Sweet Name—
   Jesus.
MOTHER:
   May the Cross protect the dead and the living!

   Neighbors, with a knife,
   With a little knife,
   On a fatal day, between two and three o'clock,
   The two men killed each other, over love.
   With a knife, with a little knife
   That scarcely fits the hand,
   But penetrates precisely
   Through the astonished flesh
   To stop exactly at the place
   Where, trembling and entangled,
   Lies the dark root of the scream.
BRIDE:
   And this is a knife,
   A little knife
   That scarcely fits the hand,
   Fish without scales or river.
   So on a fatal day, between two and three o'clock,
   With this knife
   Two men are left dead,
   With their lips turning yellow.
MOTHER:
   And it scarcely fits the hand,
   But penetrates so coldly
   Through the astonished flesh,
   And stops there—at the place

Where, trembling and entangled,
Lies the dark root of the scream.

(The NEIGHBORS, *kneeling on the ground, weep.)*

CURTAIN

YERMA

YERMA

∽∽∽

Cast of Characters

YERMA
JUAN
MARIA
VICTOR
FIRST OLD WOMAN
FIRST YOUNG WOMAN
SECOND YOUNG WOMAN
FIRST WOMAN
SECOND WOMAN
THIRD WOMAN
FOURTH WOMAN
FIFTH WOMAN
SIXTH WOMAN
FIRST SISTER

SECOND SISTER
DOLORES THE CONJURER
SECOND OLD WOMAN
THIRD OLD WOMAN
CHILDREN
BOY
FIRST MAN
SECOND MAN
THIRD MAN
YOUNGER SISTER-IN-LAW
OLDER SISTER-IN-LAW
MALE
FEMALE

ACT I

∽∽∽

SCENE 1

When the curtain rises, YERMA *is asleep with a sewing basket at her feet. There is a strange, dreamlike light. A* SHEPHERD *tiptoes in, staring at* YERMA. *He leads a* CHILD *dressed in white by the hand. The clock strikes. When the* SHEPHERD *and* CHILD *exit, the light changes to the cheerfulness of a spring morning.* YERMA *wakes up.*

VOICE: *(singing offstage)*
    Nana, Nana, Nana,
    Nana, you will see—
    We will build a little nest,
    And that's where we will be.
YERMA: Juan, do you hear me? Juan!
JUAN: Coming.
YERMA: It's time.
JUAN: Have the oxen gone by?
YERMA: Yes, they have.
JUAN: See you later. *(He starts to leave.)*
YERMA: Don't you want a glass of milk?
JUAN: What for?
YERMA: You work hard, and you aren't strong enough for so much
    work.

79

JUAN: When men stay lean, they get as strong as steel.

YERMA: But not you. When we got married, you were different. Now your face is pale—as if the sun never touched it. I wish you'd go down to the river and swim, and go up on the roof when the rain is pouring down on our house. Twenty-four months we've been married, and you keep growing sadder, thinner—as if you were growing backwards.

JUAN: Have you finished?

YERMA: *(standing up)* Don't take it wrong. If I were sick, I'd want you to take care of me. "My wife is sick. I'm going to kill this lamb to make a good meat stew." "My wife is sick. I'm going to save this chicken fat to rub on her chest." "I'm going to take her this sheepskin to wrap around her feet when it's cold." That's the way I am. That's why I take care of you.

JUAN: And I'm grateful.

YERMA: But you won't let yourself be taken care of.

JUAN: Because there's nothing wrong with me. You're just imagining all these things. I work hard. Every year I will get older.

YERMA: Every year . . . You and I will go on living here every year . . .

JUAN: *(smiling)* Of course. And very peacefully. My work goes well, and we have no children to waste money on.

YERMA: We have no children—Juan!

JUAN: Yes.

YERMA: Do you think I don't love you?

JUAN: You love me.

YERMA: I know girls who trembled and cried before they got into bed with their husbands. Did I cry the first time I went to bed with you? Wasn't I singing as I lifted the linen sheets? Didn't I say to you, "These sheets smell just like apples!"

JUAN: That's what you said.

YERMA: My mother cried because I didn't mind leaving her. And it was true. No one was ever happier to get married. And yet . . .

JUAN: Stop it! It's hard enough for me to hear all the time . . .

YERMA: Don't! Don't keep telling me what people are saying! I

can see with my own eyes that it's not true—that when the
rain falls on the rocks, they soften and make the wild mustard
grow, and people say it's useless. "Wild mustard is useless," but
I can clearly see its yellow blossoms moving in the breeze.

JUAN: You have to wait!

YERMA: Yes! Wanting!

(Taking the initiative, YERMA *embraces her husband and kisses
him.)*

JUAN: If you need anything, let me know, and I'll bring it. You
know I don't like you going out.

YERMA: I never go out.

JUAN: You're better off here.

YERMA: Yes.

JUAN: The streets are for people with nothing to do.

YERMA: *(somberly)* Of course.

(Her husband exits and YERMA *starts toward her sewing, stroking
her stomach with her hand. Stretching her arms, she yawns grace-
fully and sits down to sew.)*

YERMA:
    Where are you coming from, love, my child?
    "From the ice at the mountain's crest."
    What do you need, my love, my child?
    "To be warmed by the cloth of your dress."

(She threads her needle.)
    Let the trees lift their branches up to the sun!
    Let the waterfall leap, and the river run!

(then, as if speaking to a child)
    The dog is barking, out in the patio.
    The wind in the trees is singing, there.

The oxen follow the herder, lowing,
And the moon is weaving braids in my hair.
What do you ask for, child, from so far?

(She pauses.)
"Your breast, as white as the snow on the mountain."

Let the trees lift their branches up to the sun!
Let the waterfall leap, and the river run!

(She sews.)
I tell you, my child—it's true, it's true:
I am broken and torn for you.
My womb aches for you—
An empty cradle, craving you.

When, my child, are you going to come?

(She pauses.)
"When your flesh smells like jasmine smells."

Let the trees lift their branches up to the sun!
Let the waterfall leap, and the river run!

*(YERMA goes on singing. MARIA enters through the door with a
bundle of clothes.)*

YERMA: Where are you coming from?
MARIA: From the store.
YERMA: From the store, so early?
MARIA: If I had my way, I'd have been waiting at the door when
they opened. You'll never guess what I bought!
YERMA: You probably bought coffee for breakfast, sugar, rolls.
MARIA: No! I bought lace, three spools of thread, ribbon, and col-
ored yarn to make tassels. My husband had some money put
aside, and he himself gave it to me.
YERMA: Are you going to make a blouse?
MARIA: No, it's because—you know?

YERMA: What?

MARIA: Because it's finally happened. *(She lowers her head.* YERMA *rises and gazes at her in admiration.)*

YERMA: In five months!

MARIA: Yes.

YERMA: Can you tell it's there?

MARIA: Of course.

YERMA: *(with curiosity)* And what are you feeling?

MARIA: I don't know. Anxious.

YERMA: Anxious? *(grasping her)* But—when it happened . . . ? Tell me! You got carried away.

MARIA: Yes, carried away . . .

YERMA: You must have been singing, yes? I sing. You . . . tell me . . .

MARIA: Don't ask me. Haven't you ever had a live bird held tight in your hand?

YERMA: Yes.

MARIA: Well, it's the same—but inside your blood.

YERMA: How beautiful! *(She stares at her in wonder.)*

MARIA: I'm in a daze. I don't know anything.

YERMA: About what?

MARIA: About what I should do! I'll ask my mother.

YERMA: What for? She's old now, and she must have forgotten all that. Don't move around too much, and when you breathe, breathe as softly as if you had a rose between your teeth.

MARIA: Listen, they say that later on he pushes you gently with his little legs.

YERMA: And that's when you love him the most—when at last you say, "My son!"

MARIA: Just the same, I feel embarrassed.

YERMA: What did your husband say?

MARIA: Nothing.

YERMA: Does he love you very much?

MARIA: He doesn't tell me so, but he comes close to me and his eyes gleam like two green leaves.

YERMA: Did he know when you . . .

MARIA: Yes.

YERMA: How could he tell?

MARIA: I don't know. But on our wedding night he kept saying it, over and over, with his mouth pressed to my cheek—so many times that I feel as if my child is a fiery dove that he slipped into my ear.

YERMA: You are fortunate!

MARIA: But you know more about this than I do.

YERMA: What good does it do me?

MARIA: That's true! Why is that? Of all the girls that got married when you did, you're the only one who . . .

YERMA: That's how it is. Of course, there's still time. It took Elena three years, and in my mother's day it used to take some women much longer. But two years and twenty days, like me, is too long to wait! I don't think it's fair for me to waste away here. Many nights I go out on the patio—barefoot, to feel the earth under my feet—and I don't know why. If I go on like this, I'll come to a bad end.

MARIA: Now, look here, child! You are talking like an old woman. Listen to me. You can't complain about these things. My mother's sister had one after fourteen years—and if you could have seen the beauty of that child!

YERMA: (*eagerly*) What did he do?

MARIA: He howled like a young bull, as loud as a thousand cicadas singing at once! And he wet all over us and pulled on our braids! And when he was four months old, he covered our faces with scratches!

YERMA: (*laughing*) But those things don't hurt!

MARIA: I'll tell you—

YERMA: Bah! I've seen my sister feeding her baby with her breast covered with scratches, and it was very painful. But it was good pain—fresh, new, necessary for health.

MARIA: They say children cause a lot of suffering.

YERMA: That's a lie! Mothers who say that are weaklings, complainers! Why do they have them? Having a child is no bouquet of roses! We have to suffer for them to grow up. It must drain half of our blood. But that's good, healthy, beautiful! Every woman has enough blood for four or five children, and if she doesn't have them, it turns to poison, as it will with me.

MARIA: I don't know what's wrong with me.

YERMA: I always heard that the first time is frightening.

MARIA: *(timidly)* We'll see . . . Since you sew so well . . .

YERMA: *(taking the bundle)* Give it to me. I'll make two little suits for you. What is this?

MARIA: Those are the diapers.

YERMA: Good. *(She sits down.)*

MARIA: Then . . . I'll see you later. *(She approaches* YERMA, *who places both hands lovingly on her stomach.)*

YERMA: Don't go running on thc cobblestones.

MARIA: Good-bye! *(She kisses her and goes out.)*

YERMA: Come back soon. (YERMA *is left as we found her at the beginning. She takes the scissors and starts to cut.* VICTOR *enters.)* Hello, Victor!

VICTOR: *(He is intense and grave.)* Where is Juan?

YERMA: In the fields . . .

VICTOR: What are you making?

YERMA: I'm cutting some diapers.

VICTOR: *(smiling)* You are?

YERMA: *(laughing)* I'm going to edge them with lace.

VICTOR: If it's a girl, she'll have your name.

YERMA: *(trembling)* What?

VICTOR: I'm happy for you.

YERMA: *(almost choking)* No—they're not for me! They're for Maria's baby.

VICTOR: Well then, let's see you follow her example. This house needs a child.

YERMA: It does!

VICTOR: Then go ahead! Tell your husband to think less about his work. He wants to save money and he will, but who will he leave it to when he dies? I'm going out to the sheep. Tell Juan to pick up the two he bought from me. And as for the other— never say never! *(He exits smiling.)*

YERMA: *(passionately)*
   That's it! Never say never!
   I tell you, my child, it's true, it's true!
   I am broken and torn for you!
   My womb aches for you,
   An empty cradle, craving you.
   When, my child, are you going to come?

   "When your flesh smells like jasmine smells."

(YERMA rises pensively and goes to the spot where VICTOR stood. She takes a deep breath as if inhaling mountain air, then goes to the other side of the house as if seeking something and from there returns to sit down and pick up her sewing again. She begins to sew, but stops with her eyes fixed on one stitch.)

CURTAIN

ACT I

∽∽∽

SCENE 2

In the fields. YERMA *enters. She is carrying a basket. The* FIRST OLD WOMAN *enters.*

YERMA: Good day!

FIRST OLD WOMAN: And a good one to you, pretty miss! Where are you going?

YERMA: I've just taken food to my husband. He's working in the olive groves.

FIRST OLD WOMAN: Have you been married long?

YERMA: Three years.

FIRST OLD WOMAN: Do you have children?

YERMA: No.

FIRST OLD WOMAN: Bah! You will have.

YERMA: *(eagerly)* Do you think so?

FIRST OLD WOMAN: Why not? *(She sits down.)* I've just taken food to my husband, too. He's an old man. He still works. I have nine children, like nine shining suns, but since none of them is a girl, here I am, running from one side to the other.

YERMA: You live on the other side of the river?

FIRST OLD WOMAN: Yes, over by the windmills. Who is your family?

YERMA: I'm the daughter of Enrique, the shepherd.

FIRST OLD WOMAN: Ah! Enrique the shepherd. I knew him! Good people. Get out of bed, work hard, eat some bread, and die. No games, no nothing! Country fairs are for others. Creatures of silence. I could have married one of your uncles! But no! I have always been a woman with her skirts in the air! I went straight for the slice of melon, the fiesta, the sugar bun! I've often stuck my head out the door at daybreak, thinking I heard the sound of a fiddle coming and going—but it was only the breeze! *(She laughs.)* You are going to laugh at me. I've had two husbands and fourteen children. Five died, and in spite of that, I'm not sad and I'd like to live a lot longer! That's what I say! Fig trees—how long they last! Houses—how long they last! And only we confounded women are ground to dust by anything at all!

YERMA: I'd like to ask you a question.

FIRST OLD WOMAN: You would? *(She looks at her.)* I already know what you're going to say. It's not possible to talk about these things. *(She gets up.)*

YERMA: *(detaining her)* Why not? It's given me confidence to hear you speak. For some time, I've been wanting to have a talk with an older woman. Because I want to know. Yes! You will tell me . . .

FIRST OLD WOMAN: What?

YERMA: *(lowering her voice)* What you know. Why am I barren? Am I going to spend my best years feeding birds and hanging starched curtains in my window? No! You must tell me what I have to do, and I'll do whatever it is, even if you make me stick needles in the most sensitive part of my eyes!

FIRST OLD WOMAN: Me? I don't know anything! I used to lie on my back and begin to sing. The children came like water. Ah! Could anyone say you don't have a beautiful body? Just step out the door, and down the street a horse will whinny! Oh, leave me alone, child! Don't make me talk. I have a lot of ideas I don't want to talk about.

YERMA: Why not? With my husband, I don't talk about anything else.

FIRST OLD WOMAN: Tell me—do you like your husband?

YERMA: What?

FIRST OLD WOMAN: Do you love him? Do you want to be with him?

YERMA: I don't know.

FIRST OLD WOMAN: Don't you tremble when he comes near you? Don't you go into a trance when he brings his lips close to yours? Tell me.

YERMA: No. I have never felt like that.

FIRST OLD WOMAN: Never? Not even when you danced?

YERMA: (recalling) Perhaps. One time . . . Victor . . .

FIRST OLD WOMAN: Go on.

YERMA: . . . took me by the waist, and I couldn't say anything to him because I couldn't talk. Another time, this same Victor— fourteen years old, and big for his age—took me in his arms to help me over a ditch, and I began to tremble so hard my teeth rattled! But I've always been shy.

FIRST OLD WOMAN: What about with your husband . . . ?

YERMA: My husband is another matter. My father brought him to me, and I accepted him. Happily! That's the simple truth! From the first day we were engaged, I began to think about having children. And I saw myself reflected in his eyes. But like a very little girl, very manageable—as if I were my own daugh- ter.

FIRST OLD WOMAN: Just the opposite of me! Perhaps that's why you haven't had a baby yet. Men should be enjoyed, my child! They should undo our braids and give us water to drink from their own mouths. That's what makes the world go round!

YERMA: Yours, but not mine. I have so many dreams, and I'm sure that my son will make those dreams come true. For his sake, I gave myself to my husband, and I keep giving myself to make sure he's on the way—but never for my own pleasure!

FIRST OLD WOMAN: And the result is, you're empty!

YERMA: No, not empty—I'm filling up with hate! Tell me: is it my fault? Must you look for a man to be a man, nothing more? Then, what are you going to think when he leaves you lying in bed with sad eyes, staring at the ceiling while he turns over and goes to sleep? Should I lie there thinking about him—or about what can come shining out of my breast? I don't know, but you tell me, I beg you! *(She kneels.)*

FIRST OLD WOMAN: Oh, what a flower in full bloom! What a beautiful creature you are! Leave me alone! Don't make me talk any more. I don't want to talk to you any more! It's a question of honor, and I don't belittle anyone's honor! You'll find out. Anyway, you shouldn't be so innocent!

YERMA: *(sadly)* All the doors are closed to girls like me, who grow up in the country. Everything is half said, indicated, telling us we're not supposed to know about such things. And you, too— you, too, keep silent and put on the air of a sage—knowing everything, but denying it to a woman who is dying of thirst.

FIRST OLD WOMAN: I could talk to another woman who was more serene. Not to you! I'm old, and I know what I'm saying.

YERMA: Then God help me!

FIRST OLD WOMAN: Not God. I never cared for God. When are you going to realize that He doesn't exist? It's men who have to help you!

YERMA: But why are you telling me this, why?

FIRST OLD WOMAN: *(leaving)* Though there should be a God, if only a little one, to throw thunderbolts at men whose worthless seed dampens the pleasures of the fields!

YERMA: I don't understand what you are trying to tell me.

FIRST OLD WOMAN: Well, *I* understand! Don't get depressed. Keep your hopes up. You're still very young. What do you expect me to do?

(She leaves. TWO YOUNG WOMEN *appear.)*

FIRST YOUNG WOMAN: Wherever we go, we keep running into people!

YERMA: The men are all working out in the olive groves, and you have to take them something to eat. No one stays home except the old people.

SECOND YOUNG WOMAN: Are you going back to the village?

YERMA: That's where I'm going.

FIRST YOUNG WOMAN: I'm in a big hurry. I left my little boy asleep and there's no one home.

YERMA: Then get going, woman! Children can't be left alone. Are there pigs at your house?

FIRST YOUNG WOMAN: No, but you're right. I'll hurry!

YERMA: Go! That's how things can happen! Surely you left him locked in?

FIRST YOUNG WOMAN: Of course.

YERMA: Yes, but you don't realize what a small child is like. Something that seems so harmless to us could kill him! A tiny needle, a sip of water.

FIRST YOUNG WOMAN: You're right! I'll run. I never really think of such things. (*She exits.*)

YERMA: Go!

SECOND YOUNG WOMAN: If you had four or five, you wouldn't talk like that.

YERMA: Why not? Even if I had forty!

SECOND YOUNG WOMAN: Anyway, since you and I don't have any, we live more peacefully.

YERMA: Not me.

SECOND YOUNG WOMAN: I do! What a nuisance! On the other hand, my mother does nothing but give me herbs to make me pregnant, and in October we're going to see the Saint—the one who gives babies to any girl who begs eagerly. My mother will beg. Not me!

YERMA: Why did you get married?

SECOND YOUNG WOMAN: Because they married me off. Everybody gets married! If we go on like this, no one will be left single except the children! Well, anyway—the fact is, a girl gets married long before she goes to the church. But the old women are dead set on all of this. I'm nineteen years old, and I don't like to cook or clean. Well, now I have to spend the whole day doing things I don't like! And what for? Why is it necessary for my husband to be my husband? We did the same thing when we were engaged that we do now. Old people's foolishness!

YERMA: Hush! Don't say such things!

SECOND YOUNG WOMAN: You'll call me crazy, too! Crazy, crazy! *(She laughs.)* I can tell you the only thing I've learned in life: all the women are stuck inside their houses doing things they don't enjoy. You're better off out in the middle of the street! Sometimes I go down to the river, sometimes I climb up and ring the church bells, and sometimes I drink a little anisette.

YERMA: You're a child.

SECOND YOUNG WOMAN: Of course, but I'm not crazy! *(She laughs.)*

YERMA: Doesn't your mother live up at the top of the village?

SECOND YOUNG WOMAN: Yes.

YERMA: In the last house?

SECOND YOUNG WOMAN: Yes.

YERMA: What's her name?

SECOND YOUNG WOMAN: Dolores. Why do you ask?

YERMA: No reason.

SECOND YOUNG WOMAN: You must have some reason.

YERMA: I don't know . . . People say . . .

SECOND YOUNG WOMAN: Whatever . . . Look, I'm going to take my husband his food. *(She laughs.)* Isn't that something! It's too bad I can't say "my sweetheart," isn't it? *(She laughs.)* Here goes the crazy one! *(She leaves, laughing happily.)* Bye!

VICTOR'S VOICE: *(singing)*
Why are you sleeping alone, Shepherd?
Why are you sleeping alone, Shepherd?
My blanket is wool.
My blanket is warm.
Why are you sleeping alone, Shepherd?

YERMA: *(as she listens)*
Why are you sleeping alone, Shepherd?
My blanket is wool.

My blanket is warm.
Why do you lie on the stones, Shepherd,
With only a cover of frost, Shepherd,
And winter reeds
Your bed at night.
The needles from the oak, Shepherd,
A pillow for your head, Shepherd.
And if you hear a woman's voice,
It's the broken voice of water.
Shepherd, Shepherd.
What does the mountain want, Shepherd?
There are bitter weeds on the hill.
What child is killing you?
There are sharp thorns on the hill.

(YERMA *starts to go, but meets* VICTOR *as he enters.*)

VICTOR: *(cheerfully)* Where is this beauty going?
YERMA: Was that you singing?
VICTOR: It was.
YERMA: And so well! I never heard you sing before.
VICTOR: No?
YERMA: What a strong voice! Like a gush of water filling your
   whole mouth.
VICTOR: I'm a happy person.
YERMA: That's true.
VICTOR: As you are sad.
YERMA: I'm not a sad person, but I have enough reason to be.
VICTOR: And your husband is sadder than you are.
YERMA: Yes, he is. That's his nature.
VICTOR: He was always like that. *(He pauses.* YERMA *sits down.)*
   You came to bring his dinner?
YERMA: Yes. *(She looks at him. There is a pause.)* What do you
   have there? *(pointing to his face)*
VICTOR: Where?

YERMA: *(rising and approaching* VICTOR*)* Here—on your cheek.
    Like a burn.
VICTOR: It's nothing.
YERMA: That's what it looks like to me. *(There is a pause.)*
VICTOR: It must be the sun.
YERMA: Perhaps.

(There is a pause. The silence grows. Then, with no outward sign, an intense struggle between the two begins.)

YERMA: *(trembling)* Do you hear that?
VICTOR: What?
YERMA: Don't you hear crying?
VICTOR: *(listening)* No.
YERMA: I thought I heard a child crying.
VICTOR: Yes?
YERMA: Close by. Crying as if he were suffocating!
VICTOR: There are always lots of children around here who come
    to steal fruit.
YERMA: No. It was a baby's voice.

(There is a pause.)

VICTOR: I don't hear anything.
YERMA: It must be my imagination.

(She stares at him. VICTOR *stares back, then slowly turns away as if afraid.* JUAN *enters.)*

JUAN: What are you still doing here?
YERMA: Talking.
VICTOR: Stay well! *(He leaves.)*
JUAN: You should be at home.
YERMA: I stopped for a moment.
JUAN: I don't see why you should stop.
YERMA: I heard the birds singing.

JUAN: Oh, fine! That's how you start people talking!
YERMA: *(strongly)* Juan, what are you thinking?
JUAN: I'm not talking about you. I'm talking about other people.
YERMA: To hell with other people!
JUAN: Don't swear! It's ugly in a woman.
YERMA: How I wish I *were* a woman!
JUAN: Let's stop this conversation. Go home!

(There is a pause.)

YERMA: Very well. Should I expect you?
JUAN: No. I'll be watering the crops all night. We've had so little
    rain, and it's my turn until sunrise. And I have to stand guard
    against thieves. You go to bed and go to sleep!
YERMA: *(dramatically)* I will sleep! *(She leaves.)*

CURTAIN

END OF ACT I

ACT II

⟨⟨⟨

SCENE 1

The WOMEN *of the town are doing their washing at the river, sitting on various levels of its banks. They are singing.*

ALL:
  In the icy river,
  Washing your sash.
  Hot as a jasmine flower,
  I hear your laugh.
FIRST WOMAN: I don't like to gossip.
THIRD WOMAN: But we all gossip here.
FOURTH WOMAN: And there's no harm in it.
FIFTH WOMAN: A woman who wants a good reputation has to
  earn it.
FOURTH WOMAN:
  I planted some thyme seeds.
  See how they grew!
  If you want a good name,
  Take care what you do!

(They laugh.)

FIFTH WOMAN: That's what they say!

96

FIRST WOMAN: But you never really know.

FOURTH WOMAN: We do know her husband has brought his two sisters in to live with them.

FIFTH WOMAN: The old maids?

FOURTH WOMAN: Yes. They used to be in charge of keeping an eye on the church. Now they'll be keeping an eye on their sister-in-law! I wouldn't be able to live with them!

FIRST WOMAN: Why?

FOURTH WOMAN: Because they are frightening! They are like those enormous leaves that suddenly sprout up out of graves. They're smeared with wax! Stuffed up inside! They probably cook their food in kerosene!

THIRD WOMAN: Are they already at the house?

FOURTH WOMAN: Since yesterday. The husband is going out to his fields again.

FIRST WOMAN: Can you just tell me what happened?

FIFTH WOMAN: She spent the night before last sitting on the doorstep, in spite of the cold!

FIRST WOMAN: But why?

FOURTH WOMAN: It's hard for her to stay in the house!

FIFTH WOMAN: These barren women are like that. When they could be making lace or apple preserves, they like to go up on the roof or walk barefoot along some river!

FIRST WOMAN: Who are you to say such things? She has no children, but that's not her fault!

FOURTH WOMAN: You have children if you *want* to have them! These spoiled, weak, lazy women were never meant to have wrinkles on their bellies!

(*They laugh.*)

THIRD WOMAN: They put on face powder and rouge, and they wear a sprig of oleander in pursuit of a man who is not their husband!

FIFTH WOMAN: Nothing could be truer!

FIRST WOMAN: But have any of you seen her with another man?

FOURTH WOMAN: We haven't, but other people have!

FIRST WOMAN: Always other people!

FIFTH WOMAN: They say it happened on two occasions.

SECOND WOMAN: And what were they doing?

FOURTH WOMAN: Talking.

FIRST WOMAN: Talking is not a sin!

FOURTH WOMAN: There's something in this world called a "look." My mother used to say that. A woman doesn't look at roses the same way she looks at a man's trousers. She "looks" at him!

FIRST WOMAN: But at who?

FOURTH WOMAN: At someone, do you hear? Can you get that into your head, or do I have to say it louder? *(laughter)* And when she's not looking at him because she's alone, because he's not right there in front of her, she has his picture in her mind's eye.

FIRST WOMAN: That's a lie!

(They all laugh uproariously.)

FIFTH WOMAN: What about the husband?

THIRD WOMAN: The husband acts like he's deaf. He does nothing, like a lizard left in the sun.

(They laugh.)

FIRST WOMAN: All this could be straightened out if they had children.

SECOND WOMAN: All this is what happens to people who don't accept their fate.

FOURTH WOMAN: Every hour that passes makes that house more like hell! All day long without ever speaking to each other, she and his sisters whitewash the walls, scour the copper, steam the windows clean, polish the floors! And the more that house sparkles, the more like an inferno it becomes!

FIRST WOMAN: It's his fault, his! If a man can't give his wife children, he'd better keep an eye on her.

FOURTH WOMAN: It's her fault. She has a tongue that could sharpen knives!

FIRST WOMAN: What the devil has got into your head to make you talk like that?

FOURTH WOMAN: Who gave your mouth a license to give me advice?

SECOND WOMAN: Be quiet!

FIRST WOMAN: I'd like to string your muttering tongues on a knitting needle!

SECOND WOMAN: Shut up!

FOURTH WOMAN: And me, the tits of the hypocrites!

SECOND WOMAN: Hush! Don't you see his sisters are coming this way? (*They whisper together.*)

(YERMA's *two* SISTERS-IN-LAW *enter. They're wearing mourning. In the silence, they begin to wash their clothes. There is the sound of sheep bells.*)

FIRST WOMAN: Are the shepherds leaving now?

THIRD WOMAN: Yes, now all the flocks will be leaving.

FOURTH WOMAN: (*inhaling*) I love the smell of sheep.

THIRD WOMAN: You do?

FOURTH WOMAN: And why not? The smell of what's yours! Just as I like the smell of the red clay the river brings in the winter.

THIRD WOMAN: What strange ideas!

FIFTH WOMAN: (*looking out*) The flocks are all leaving together.

FOURTH WOMAN: It's a flood of wool! Sweeping over everything! If the green wheat knew what was coming, how it would tremble!

THIRD WOMAN: Look at them run! What a herd of devils!

FIRST WOMAN: Now they're all out. Not one is missing.

FOURTH WOMAN: Let's see . . . no . . . Yes, yes, one is missing!

FIFTH WOMAN: Which?

FOURTH WOMAN: Victor's.

(*The two* SISTERS-IN-LAW *sit up and look out.*)

FOURTH WOMAN:
> In the icy river
> I wash your sash.
> Hot as a jasmine flower
> Is your laugh.
> I want to live
> In the tiny snowdrift
> Of that jasmine.

FIRST WOMAN:
> Alas, for the barren woman!
> Alas, for the wife with breasts of sand!

FIFTH WOMAN:
> Tell me if your husband
> Still has seed
> To send the water singing
> Through your sheets.

FOURTH WOMAN:
> Your sheets are a boat
> Made of silver and wind,
> On the edge of the stream.

FIRST WOMAN:
> I come to the river washing
> The clothes of my son,
> To teach the crystal waters
> To shine and run!

SECOND WOMAN:
> He is coming from the mountain,
> My husband, to eat.
> He's bringing me a rosebud,
> And I will give him three.

FIFTH WOMAN:
> He is coming from the lowland,
> My husband, to sup.
> He's bringing me hot embers,
> Which I will cover up.

FOURTH WOMAN:
He is coming on the breezes,
My husband, to bed.
My violets are crimson.
His violet is red.
FIRST WOMAN:
Join together flower with flower
When summer dries the reaper's blood.
FOURTH WOMAN:
And open your womb to sleepless birds
When winter trembles at the door.
FIRST WOMAN:
We must moan on our bedsheets!
FOURTH WOMAN:
And we must sing!
FIFTH WOMAN:
When a man is bringing
The crown and the bread.
FOURTH WOMAN:
Because our arms will interlace!
SECOND WOMAN:
Because the light bursts in our throats!
FOURTH WOMAN:
Because the green stalk becomes sweet.
FIRST WOMAN:
And a canvas of wind covers the mountain.

(SIXTH WOMAN *appears from the top of the falls.*)

SIXTH WOMAN:
And so a child conceives
Crystal shards of dawn.
FIRST WOMAN:
And our body has
Branches of raging coral.

SIXTH WOMAN:
   So that there are oarsmen
   On the waters of the sea.
FIRST WOMAN:
   A little child, a child!
SECOND WOMAN:
   And doves open their wings and beaks.
THIRD WOMAN:
   A child that howls, a son!
FOURTH WOMAN:
   And the men push forward
   Like wounded stags.
FIFTH WOMAN:
   Joyful, joyful, joyful!
   The rounded womb, under the nightgown.
SECOND WOMAN:
   Joyful, joyful, joyful!
   The navel, a tender chalice of wonder.
FIRST WOMAN:
   Alas, for the barren woman!
   Alas, for the wife with breasts of sand!
THIRD WOMAN:
   Let her shine!
SECOND WOMAN:
   Let her run!
FIFTH WOMAN:
   Let her shine again!
FIRST WOMAN:
   Let her sing!
SECOND WOMAN:
   Let her hide!
FIRST WOMAN:
   And let her sing again!
SIXTH WOMAN:
   The new dawn that my child
   Is wearing on his apron.

SECOND WOMAN: *(They all sing in chorus.)*
  In the icy river,
  I wash your sash.
  Hot as a jasmine flower
  Is your laugh.
  Ha, ha, ha!

(They move the pieces of laundry in rhythm, and beat them.)

CURTAIN

ACT II

కావావా

SCENE 2

YERMA's *house. It is growing late.* JUAN *is seated.* JUAN's *two* SISTERS *are standing.*

JUAN: You say she went out a little while ago? (*The* OLDER SISTER *nods her assent.*) She must be at the fountain. But you *know* I don't like her to go out alone. (*There is a pause.*) You can set the table. (*The* YOUNGER SISTER *exits.*) I really earn the bread I eat! (*to his* SISTER) Yesterday I had a hard day. I was pruning the apple trees and by the end of the afternoon I began to think—why am I working so hard if I can't even put one apple in my mouth? I'm fed up! (*He passes his hand over his face. There is a pause.*) She hasn't come. One of you should always go with her! That's why you're here, eating at my table and drinking my wine! My work is in the fields, but my honor is here. And my honor is yours, as well. (*The* SISTER *bows her head.*) Don't take me wrong. (YERMA *enters carrying two pitchers. She stops in the doorway.*) Have you been to the fountain?
YERMA: Yes, so we could have fresh water with our dinner. (*The* OTHER SISTER *enters.*) How are things in the fields?

(YERMA *sets down the pitchers. There is a pause.*)
104

JUAN: I spent yesterday pruning trees.

YERMA: Will you be staying?

JUAN: I have to take care of the flock. You know you have to, if you own sheep.

YERMA: I know it very well. Don't say it again!

JUAN: Every man has his work.

YERMA: And every woman, hers! I'm not asking you to stay. I have everything I need here. Your sisters watch over me very well. Here, I eat fresh bread and cheese and roast lamb, and in the mountains your sheep graze on grass washed with dew. I think you can live in peace.

JUAN: To live in peace, you have to be at peace!

YERMA: And you are not.

JUAN: I am not.

YERMA: Change your way of thinking!

JUAN: Don't you know the way I think? The sheep in the pens and the women in their houses. You're out too much! Haven't you always heard me say that?

YERMA: You're right! The women in their houses. If the houses are not tombs! If chairs get broken and cotton sheets wear out from being used! But not here! Every night when I get into bed, the bed seems to be newer, shinier, as if it had just been brought from the city.

JUAN: You yourself admit that I have reason to complain! That I have reason to be on my guard.

YERMA: On your guard against what? I don't do anything to hurt you! I am always submissive to you, and whatever I suffer, I keep to myself. And each day that goes by will be worse. Let's stop talking! I'll carry my cross the best I can, just don't ask me any questions! If I could suddenly become old, with a mouth like a crushed flower, then I could smile at you and share life with you. Now—now, leave me to my agony!

JUAN: You're talking in a way I don't understand. I deprive you of nothing! I send to nearby towns for things you like. I have my faults, but I want to have peace and quiet with you. I want to be able to sleep when I'm away and to know that you're sleeping, too!

YERMA: But I don't sleep, I can't sleep!

JUAN: Is there something you need? Tell me. Answer me!

YERMA: *(meaningfully, staring at her husband)* Yes, I need something!

(There is a pause.)

JUAN: Always the same! It's been more than five years now! I'm ready to forget about it.

YERMA: But I'm not you! Men have another life—the flocks, the orchards, the conversations! Women only have their children and caring for their children.

JUAN: Everyone is not the same. Why don't you take in one of your brother's children? I wouldn't be against it.

YERMA: I don't want to take care of other people's children! I think my arms would freeze just holding them!

JUAN: Always brooding about this is driving you crazy. You never think about the things you should, and you insist on beating your head against a rock!

YERMA: A rock that is shameful—because it *is* a rock, when it should be a basket of flowers and sweet water!

JUAN: Being around you only makes me restless and uneasy. When there's no other choice, you should resign yourself.

YERMA: I came to this house so I wouldn't have to resign myself! When I'm in my coffin with my hands tied together and a cloth wrapped around my head to keep my mouth from falling open—that's when I'll resign myself!

JUAN: Then, what do you want to do?

YERMA: I want to drink water, and there's no glass and no water! I want to climb the mountain, and I have no feet! I want to embroider my petticoats, and I can't find the thread!

JUAN: The truth is you're not a real woman—and you're trying to destroy a man who has no will of his own!

YERMA: I don't know who I am. Let me go out and walk to ease my burden! In nothing have I failed you!

JUAN: I don't like people pointing at me! That's why I want to see that door locked and each person in his house!

(FIRST SISTER *enters slowly and goes toward a cupboard.*)

YERMA: Talking to people is not a sin!

JUAN: But it can seem like one!

(*The* OTHER SISTER *enters and goes to the pitchers, from which she fills a water jug.*)

JUAN: (*lowering his voice*) I don't have the strength for all this. When people start a conversation, close your mouth and remember you're a married woman!

YERMA: (*darkly*) Married!

JUAN: And that families have their honor and honor is a burden that two people must bear!

(*The* OTHER SISTER *slowly exits with the water jug.*)

JUAN: But it grows fragile and confused inside the channels of our blood.

(*The* FIRST SISTER *exits with a tray. Her gait is almost processional. There is a pause.*)

JUAN: Forgive me.

(YERMA *looks at her husband; he raises his head and catches her glance.*)

JUAN: Though the way you are looking at me, I shouldn't say, "Forgive me." I should force you, lock you up, because that is what a husband is for!

(The two SISTERS *appear at the door.)*

YERMA: I beg you not to talk! Let the matter rest.

(There is a pause.)

JUAN: Let's eat!

(The two SISTERS *enter.)*

JUAN: Did you hear me?
YERMA: *(sweetly)* You eat with your sisters. I'm not hungry yet.
JUAN: As you wish. *(He exits.)*
YERMA: *(as if in a dream)*
    Oh, what a pasture of pain!
    Oh, the gate barred against beauty!
    I crave to carry a child, but the breeze
    Offers dahlias as dark as the dreaming moon.
    Deep in my flesh I have two warm springs,
    Two throbbing fountainheads of milk—
    The pulsing hoofbeats of a horse,
    Which palpitate upon my anguish.
    Oh, blind breasts under my clothing!
    Oh, doves without eyes, doves without whiteness!
    Oh, the stinging pain of imprisoned blood
    Nailing wasps to the nape of my neck!
    But surely you'll come, my love, my son!
    As the sea gives salt, and the earth bears grain,
    Our womb will swell with a tender child,
    Like a cloud which brings the sweet, fresh rain.

(looking toward the door) Maria, why do you pass my house in
    such a hurry?
MARIA: *(entering with a baby in her arms)* When I have the baby
    with me, I do—since you always cry!

YERMA: That's true. *(She takes the baby and sits down.)*

MARIA: It makes me sad that you feel jealous.

YERMA: I don't feel jealous—I feel deprived.

MARIA: Don't complain.

YERMA: How can I keep from complaining, when I see you and the other women in full bloom, and I see myself useless in the middle of so much beauty?

MARIA: But you have other things. If you'd listen to me, you could be happy.

YERMA: A woman from the country who doesn't bear children is as useless as a handful of thorns—even sinful! And so, I'm part of the refuse discarded by God's hand! (MARIA *reaches for the child.)* Take him, he's happier with you! I suppose I don't have a mother's hands!

MARIA: Why do you say that?

YERMA: *(getting up)* Because I'm fed up! Because I'm fed up with having them and not being able to use them for the right thing. Because I am hurt—hurt and completely degraded—watching how the wheat springs up, how the fountains never cease giving water, and how the sheep give birth to hundreds of lambs, and the dogs, and how it seems as if the whole countryside rises up to show me its young offspring, drowsily nursing, while I feel the blows of a hammer, here, where my baby's mouth should be!

MARIA: I don't like what you're saying!

YERMA: When women have children, they can't understand those who don't! You stay fresh, ignorant—like people who swim in sweet water with no idea of what thirst is.

MARIA: I don't want to say to you what I always say.

YERMA: Each time I have more need—and less hope!

MARIA: How awful!

YERMA: I'll end up believing that I'm my own son. I often go down to feed the oxen—which I never used to do because women don't—and when I walk through the dark shed, my footsteps sound to me like those of a man.

MARIA: You are what you are.

YERMA: In spite of everything, he goes on loving me. Now you see how I live!

MARIA: What about his sisters?

YERMA: I'll be dead and buried before I'll ever speak to them!

MARIA: What about your husband?

YERMA: The three of them are against me.

MARIA: What do they think?

YERMA: They imagine things. Like people with a guilty conscience. They think I could want another man. And they don't realize that even if I did, my honor comes first with me! They are stones in my path! But they don't know that if I want to, I can become a torrent of water and sweep them away!

(A SISTER *enters and then exits, carrying a loaf of bread.)*

MARIA: Anyway, I think your husband still loves you.

YERMA: My husband gives me bread and board.

MARIA: What a difficult time you're having, what a difficult time! But remember the wounds of Our Lord.

(They are at the doorway.)

YERMA: *(looking at the child)* He's awake now.

MARIA: In a little while, he'll start to sing!

YERMA: The same eyes as you, you know that? Have you seen them? *(weeping)* He has the same eyes that you have. (YERMA *gently pushes* MARIA, *who leaves in silence.* YERMA *goes toward the door through which her husband left.)*

(The SECOND YOUNG WOMAN *appears.)*

SECOND YOUNG WOMAN: Psst!

YERMA: *(turning)* What?

SECOND YOUNG WOMAN: I waited for her to leave. My mother is expecting you.

YERMA: Is she alone?
SECOND YOUNG WOMAN: Two neighbors are with her.
YERMA: Tell them to wait a bit.
SECOND YOUNG WOMAN: But are you going? Aren't you afraid?
YERMA: I am going.
SECOND YOUNG WOMAN: Whatever you say!
YERMA: Have them wait for me, even if it's late!

(VICTOR *enters.*)

VICTOR: Is Juan at home?
YERMA: Yes.
SECOND YOUNG WOMAN: *(like an accomplice)* As I was saying, I'll
    bring the blouse later.
YERMA: Whenever you like. (SECOND YOUNG WOMAN *leaves.*) Sit
    down.
VICTOR: I'm fine this way.
YERMA: *(calling)* Juan!
VICTOR: I've come to say good-bye.

(*He trembles slightly, but recovers his composure.*)

YERMA: Are you going to live with your brothers?
VICTOR: That's what my father wants.
YERMA: He must be old now.
VICTOR: Yes, very old.

(*There is a pause.*)

YERMA: A change of scenery will do you good.
VICTOR: All scenery is the same.
YERMA: No. I would go very far away.
VICTOR: It's all the same. The same sheep have the same wool.
YERMA: For men, yes; but women are another matter. I never
    heard a man who was eating say: "How good these apples are!"

You go on your way without noticing the little things. As for
me, I can say I have hated the water from these wells!

VICTOR: It could be.

(The stage is in soft shadow.)

YERMA: Victor.
VICTOR: Yes.
YERMA: Why are you leaving? Everybody here likes you.
VICTOR: I've behaved myself.

(There is a pause.)

YERMA: You've behaved. One time when you were a strong young
shepherd, you carried me in your arms, don't you remember?
You never know what's going to happen.
VICTOR: Everything changes.
YERMA: Some things don't change! There are things locked up
behind the walls that can never change because nobody hears
them!
VICTOR: That's how it is.

(The SECOND SISTER *appears and goes slowly toward the door
where she stands still, illuminated by the last light of afternoon.)*

YERMA: But if they suddenly exploded, they would shake the
world!
VICTOR: Nothing would be gained. The water in its channel, the
flock in the fold, the moon in the sky, and a man with his plow!
YERMA: What a terrible shame not to be able to learn from the
teachings of the old people!

(The long, melancholy sound of a shepherd's horn is heard.)

VICTOR: The flocks.
JUAN: *(entering)* Are you on your way now?

VICTOR: I want to get past the harbor before daybreak.

JUAN: Do I owe you anything?

VICTOR: No. You paid me well.

JUAN: *(to* YERMA*)* I bought his flocks.

YERMA: Yes?

VICTOR: *(to* YERMA*)* They're yours.

YERMA: I didn't know.

JUAN: *(with satisfaction)* It's true!

VICTOR: Your husband will see his land filled to overflowing!

YERMA: The fruits fall into the hands of the one who reaches for
them.

(The SISTER *who is at the door goes inside.)*

JUAN: Now we don't have enough land for so many sheep!

YERMA: *(sadly)* There's a lot of land!

(There is a pause.)

JUAN: We'll go together as far as the river.

VICTOR: I wish great happiness for this house!

(He shakes YERMA*'s hand.)*

YERMA: May God hear you. Stay well!

*(*VICTOR *starts to leave but after an imperceptible movement by*
YERMA, *he turns back.)*

VICTOR: Did you say something?

YERMA: *(dramatically)* I said "Stay well!"

VICTOR: Thank you.

(They leave. YERMA *is left in anguish, looking at the hand which*
VICTOR *shook. Then she quickly crosses to the left and picks up a
shawl.)*

SECOND YOUNG WOMAN: *(entering)* Let's go! *(In silence, she covers* YERMA's *head.)*
YERMA: Let's go!

(They leave stealthily. The stage is almost dark. The FIRST SISTER *enters with an oil lamp that casts only its own light on the scene. She goes to the edge of the stage looking for* YERMA. *The shepherds' horns sound.)*

FIRST SISTER: *(softly)* Yerma!

(The SECOND SISTER *enters. They look at each other and then move toward the door.)*

OTHER SISTER: *(louder)* Yerma!
FIRST SISTER: *(as she goes out the door, in an imperious voice)* YERMA!

(Shepherds' horns sound. The stage is completely dark.)

CURTAIN

END OF ACT II

ACT III

∽∽∽

SCENE 1

The house of DOLORES THE CONJURER. *Day is breaking.* YERMA *enters with* DOLORES, SECOND OLD WOMAN, *and* THIRD OLD WOMAN.

DOLORES: You were very brave!

SECOND OLD WOMAN: There's no force in the world like that of desire.

THIRD OLD WOMAN: But the cemetery was so dark!

DOLORES: I've said those prayers in the cemetery many times with women eager to have babies, and they were all afraid! All but you!

YERMA: I came for the result. I don't believe you're a deceitful woman.

DOLORES: I'm not! Let my tongue crawl with ants like the mouths of the dead, if I have ever told a lie! The last time, I said the prayer with a beggar woman who'd been empty much longer than you, and her womb sweetened so beautifully she had two babies down there by the river, because she didn't have time to get to the village, and she herself brought them in a piece of cloth for me to tend to.

YERMA: And she was able to walk here from the river?

115

DOLORES: She got here. With her shoes and her petticoats soaked with blood—but with her face shining!

YERMA: And nothing happened to her?

DOLORES: What could happen? God is God.

YERMA: Of course, God is God! Nothing could happen to her. Just pick up the babies and wash them in fresh water! Animals lick them, don't they? That wouldn't disgust me with my own child. I have the notion that women who have just given birth are glowing inside, and that their babies sleep on top of them for hours and hours, listening to the river of warm milk that goes on filling the breasts so they can suckle, so they can play until they don't want any more, until they pull their heads away. "Just a little bit more, my child . . ." And their faces and chests are covered with white drops!

DOLORES: Now you will have a child. I can assure you.

YERMA: I will have one because I must! Or I don't understand the world. Sometimes, when I'm sure I never, never . . . a wave of fire sweeps up from my feet, and leaves me empty of everything; and the men walking along the street, and the bulls, and the stones—they seem to me like things made of cotton. And I ask myself: "What are they there for?"

SECOND OLD WOMAN: It's all right for a married woman to want children, but if she doesn't have them, why this anxiety for them? What's important in this world is to get through the years. I'm not criticizing you. You saw how I helped with the praying. But what lush land do you hope to leave your son—or what good fortune—or what silver throne?

YERMA: I don't think about tomorrow, I think about today! You're old, and now you see everything like a book you've read before. I feel as if I am thirsty and I have no freedom! I want to hold my child in my arms so I can sleep peacefully! And listen carefully, and don't be frightened by what I say: even if I already knew that one day my son was going to torture me, and hate me, and drag me through the streets by the hair, I would still rejoice at his birth! It's much better to cry over a man who is alive and stabs you with a knife, than to cry over this phantom sitting on my heart, year after year!

SECOND OLD WOMAN: You're too young to listen to advice! But while you're waiting for the grace of God, you should find shelter in your husband's love.

YERMA: Ai! You've put your finger on the deepest wound in my flesh!

DOLORES: Your husband is good.

YERMA: (*She gets up.*) He is good. He is good! What of it? I wish he were bad! But no! He takes his sheep along their paths and counts his money at night. When he covers me with his body, he is doing his duty, but I feel his waist as cold as a corpse! I have always been disgusted by hot-blooded women, but at that moment I would like to be a mountain of fire!

DOLORES: Yerma!

YERMA: I'm not an unfaithful wife, but I know that children are conceived by a man and a woman. Oh, if only I could have them all by myself!

DOLORES: Think how your husband suffers, too.

YERMA: He doesn't suffer! The fact is he doesn't want children.

SECOND OLD WOMAN: Don't say that!

YERMA: I can see it in his eyes, and since he doesn't want them, he doesn't give them to me. I don't love him, I don't love him, and yet he's my only salvation! For honor and for family! My only salvation!

SECOND OLD WOMAN: (*fearfully*) Soon it will be dawn! You should go home.

DOLORES: Before you know it, the flocks will be coming out, and it's not good for you to be seen alone!

YERMA: I needed to get this off my chest. How many times do I repeat the prayers?

DOLORES: The prayer of the laurel twice—and at noon the prayer of Santa Ana. When you feel you're pregnant, bring me the bushel of wheat you promised me.

SECOND OLD WOMAN: Now it's beginning to grow light on the mountaintops. Go!

DOLORES: Any minute people will be opening their doors, so you'd better go around by the canal.

YERMA: *(disheartened)* I don't know why I came.

DOLORES: Are you sorry?

YERMA: No!

DOLORES: *(upset)* If you're afraid, I'll go with you as far as the corner.

SECOND OLD WOMAN: *(uneasily)* It will be daylight by the time you get to your door.

(VOICES are heard.)

DOLORES: Be quiet!

(They listen.)

SECOND OLD WOMAN: It's no one. God go with you!

(YERMA goes toward the door, but at that moment a knock is heard. The three women stop still.)

DOLORES: Who is it?

JUAN'S VOICE: It's me!

YERMA: Open it! (DOLORES *is unsure.*) Are you going to open it or not?

(Murmuring is heard. JUAN and his SISTERS appear.)

OTHER SISTER: Here she is!

YERMA: Here I am!

JUAN: What are you doing in this place? If I could shout, I would rouse the whole village so they could see what's become of my family honor! But I have to choke it all back and keep quiet because you are my wife.

YERMA: If I could, I would shout, too—so even the dead would rise up and see that I am cloaked in purity!

JUAN: No, not that! I can put up with anything but that! You deceive me, you confuse me, but I'm only a man who works the land, and I can't compete with your cleverness!

DOLORES: Juan!

JUAN: Not a word out of any of you!

DOLORES: *(firmly)* Your wife has done nothing wrong.

JUAN: She's been doing it since the very day of our wedding. Looking daggers at me, spending the nights on watch, lying at my side with her eyes open, and filling my pillows with her unhappy sighs!

YERMA: Shut your mouth!

JUAN: And I can't stand any more! You'd have to be made of bronze to put up with a woman at your side who wants to jab her fingers into your heart and goes out of her house at night—looking for what? Tell me! Looking for what? The streets are full of men. You don't go out on the streets to pick flowers!

YERMA: I won't let you say one more word! Not one more! You and your family think you're the only people who care about honor, and you don't know that my family has never had anything to hide. Come here! Come close to me and smell my clothing; come close! Let's see where you can find a smell that's not yours, that's not from your body! Stand me naked in the middle of the plaza, and spit on me! Do what you like with me since I'm your wife, but take care you don't put another man's name on my breast!

JUAN: It's not me who puts it there—you put it there with your behavior, and the town is beginning to talk! Beginning to talk! When I join a group of people, they all grow quiet. When I go to weigh the flour, they all grow quiet. And even at night, when I wake up in the fields, it seems as if the branches of the trees grow quiet, too!

YERMA: Those evil winds that tumble the wheat—I don't know why they start. See for yourself if the wheat is good!

JUAN: Nor do I know what a woman is looking for, out of her house at all hours!

YERMA: *(in an outburst, embracing her husband)* I'm looking for you! I'm looking for you! It's you I look for, day and night, without finding any shade where I can rest! It's your children and your help I want!

JUAN: Get away!

YERMA: Don't push me away—want *with* me!

JUAN: Stop it!

YERMA: See how alone I am! Like the moon trying to find herself in the sky. Look at me! *(She looks at him.)*

JUAN: *(looking at her, and brusquely pushing her away)* Leave me alone, once and for all!

DOLORES: Juan!

(YERMA *falls to the floor.*)

YERMA: *(loudly)* When I went out to pick my carnations, I ran into the wall. Ai! Ai! That's the wall where I have to smash my head to pieces!

JUAN: Be quiet! Let's go!

DOLORES: My God!

YERMA: *(screaming)* Damn my father for giving me his blood— the blood of the father of a hundred sons! Damn my blood that pounds on the walls looking for them!

JUAN: Be quiet, I said!

DOLORES: People are coming! Talk softly!

YERMA: I don't care! Let at least my voice be free, now that I'm falling into the darkest part of the pit! *(She gets up.)* Let my body send out at least one beautiful thing, and let it fill the air.

(VOICES *are heard.*)

DOLORES: They're going to pass by here.

JUAN: Silence!

YERMA: Of course, of course. Silence. Don't worry.

JUAN: Let's go! Quickly!

YERMA: All right! All right! But it's no use wringing my hands. Wanting something is one thing—

JUAN: Be quiet!

YERMA: Wanting something is one thing, but it's something else when your body—damn the body!—won't respond. This is my fate and I'm not going to fight against the tide. That's it! Let my lips be sealed! *(She leaves.)*

FAST CURTAIN

ACT III

∽∾∽

SCENE 2

*On the grounds of a shrine, high in the mountains. Downstage,
the wheels of a cart and some blankets form a crude tent where*
YERMA *sits. The* WOMEN *enter, bringing offerings to the shrine.
They are barefoot. In the group is the spirited* FIRST OLD WOMAN
from the first act.

VOICES: *(singing offstage)*
    I couldn't see you
    When you were single,
    But now you're married;
    I will find you.
    I'll strip you naked,
    Wife and pilgrim,
    When, in the dark,
    It's striking twelve.
FIRST OLD WOMAN: *(lazily)* Did you drink the holy water yet?
FIRST WOMAN: Yes.
FIRST OLD WOMAN: And now, we'll see about this one.
FIRST WOMAN: We believe in him.
FIRST OLD WOMAN: You all come to ask the Saint to give you
    children, and the result is that each year more single men come
    on this pilgrimage. What is going on? *(She laughs.)*

122

FIRST WOMAN: Why do you come here if you don't believe?

FIRST OLD WOMAN: To watch. It drives me crazy to watch! And to look after my son. Last year two men killed each other over one of these barren wives, and I want to keep an eye on him. And finally, I come because I feel like it!

FIRST WOMAN: May God forgive you!

(They exit.)

FIRST OLD WOMAN: *(sarcastically)* May He forgive you! *(She leaves.)*

(MARIA *and the* FIRST YOUNG WOMAN *enter.)*

FIRST YOUNG WOMAN: Has she come?

MARIA: There is her cart. I had a hard time getting them to come. For the past month, she hasn't been out of her chair. She frightens me! She has something in mind; I don't know what it is, but you can be sure it's nothing good!

FIRST YOUNG WOMAN: I came with my sister. She's been coming for eight years without results.

MARIA: You have children if you are meant to have them.

FIRST YOUNG WOMAN: That's what I say!

(There are VOICES *offstage.)*

MARIA: I never liked this pilgrimage! Let's go into the wheat shed, that's where everyone is!

FIRST YOUNG WOMAN: Last year when it got dark, some young men were pinching my sister's breasts!

MARIA: For four leagues around, you hear nothing but filthy language!

FIRST YOUNG WOMAN: I saw more than forty barrels of wine in back of the shrine!

MARIA: A river of men without women flows down these mountains!

(They exit. Offstage VOICES. YERMA *enters with six* WOMEN *who are going to the church. They carry decorated candles. Dusk begins to fall.)*

YERMA:
Lord, let all the roses bloom,
Don't leave mine in the shade!
SECOND WOMAN:
Upon your barren flesh
The yellow rose will bloom.
YERMA:
And in the womb of your servants,
The dark flame of the earth.
CHORUS OF WOMEN:
Lord, let all the roses bloom,
Don't leave mine in the shade!

(They kneel.)

YERMA:
Heaven is full of gardens
With roses of happiness,
And there among the roses
Is one miraculous rose.
It shines like a ray of aurora,
An archangel guards it well,
With wings like enormous storm clouds,
And eyes like agonies.
And all around its petals,
Rivers of sweet, warm milk
Flow and bathe the faces
Of the tranquil stars.
Lord, open your rose
Upon my barren flesh!

(They get up.)

SECOND WOMAN:
> Lord, cool with your hand
> The burning coals of my cheek!

YERMA:
> Listen to the penitent
> On your holy pilgrimage.
> Open your rose in my flesh,
> The rose with a thousand thorns.

CHORUS OF WOMEN:
> Lord, let all the roses bloom,
> Don't leave mine in the shade!

YERMA:
> Over my barren flesh,
> One miraculous rose!

(They exit. YOUNG GIRLS *come running out from the left with long garlands in their hands. From the right, three* OTHERS, *looking back over their shoulders. There is a crescendo of shouting and the sounds of bells and harness bells. On an upper level, the seven* YOUNG GIRLS *wave their garlands toward the left. The racket increases, as two mummers enter, one as a* MALE, *the other as a* FEMALE. *They wear large folk masks. The* MALE *clutches the horn of a bull in his hand. They are not grotesque in any way, but are of great beauty and pure earthiness. The* FEMALE *shakes a strap of large harness bells. Upstage, a crowd of* PEOPLE *shout and cheer the dancers on. Night has fallen.)*

CHILDREN: The devil and his wife! The devil and his wife!

FEMALE:
> In the river in the mountains,
> The despondent wife was bathing.
> Up along her naked body,
> Tiny water snails were climbing.
> The sand along the river edge,
> The breeze of early morning,
> Set her laughter all afire,

Made her shoulders tremble.
Oh, she was naked and laughing,
The maiden in the water!

BOY:
Oh, how she was moaning!

FIRST MAN:
Oh, thirsty for loving!
Dry, in the wind and the water!

SECOND MAN:
Who is the one you're awaiting?

FIRST MAN:
Who is the one that you watch for?

SECOND MAN:
Oh, with your womb that is empty,
And with your color fading!

FEMALE:
When night has come, I'll say it.
When night has come, transparent,
When night has come to the ritual,
I'll tear my petticoats open!

BOY:
And night was falling quickly.
Oh, how the night was falling!
See how the darkness gathers
At the waterfall on the mountain.

(*Guitars begin to play.*)

MALE: (*rising and shaking the horns*)
Oh, the purity
Of the despondent wife!
Oh, how she moans among the branches!
Later, she will be a poppy, a carnation—
Later, when the male unfolds his cape.

(*He comes nearer.*)

If you come to the ritual—

Come to pray that your womb will open—
Don't put on a veil of mourning,
Wear your softest, finest linen.
Go behind the walls alone,
Where the secret fires are hidden,
Tolerate my earthly body,
Till the first white sigh of daybreak.
Oh, how she is glowing!
Oh, how she was glowing!
Oh, how the wife is throbbing!

FEMALE:

Oh, how love endows her
With garlands and with crowns;
And darts of molten gold
Penetrate her breast!

MALE:

Seven times she moaned, and
Nine times she rose, and
Fifteen times the jasmine
Fused with the orange.

THIRD MAN:

Again, now use the horn!

SECOND MAN:

Again, the rose, the dance!

FIRST MAN:

Oh, how the wife is throbbing!

MALE:

In this ritual,
The male always leads.
Married men are bulls.
The male always leads.
Now, give the wreath
And the pilgrim flowers
To the man who wins them!

BOY:

Again, now with the wind!

SECOND MAN:
Again, now with the wreath!
MALE:
Come and see the glow
Of the wife who was bathing!
FIRST MAN:
She bends like a reed.
FEMALE:
She fades like a flower.
MEN:
Let the little girls leave!
MALE:
Let them burn: the dance
And the glowing body
Of the innocent wife!

(*They are dancing off, smiling, to the sound of handclaps. They sing.*)
Heaven is full of gardens,
With roses of happiness.
And there among the roses
Is one miraculous rose.

(*Two* YOUNG WOMEN *go by again, shouting. The cheerful* FIRST OLD WOMAN *enters.*)

FIRST OLD WOMAN:
We'll see if you let us sleep later on! But later on, it will be her turn! (YERMA *enters.*) You! (YERMA *is downcast and does not speak.*) Tell me, why did you come?
YERMA:
I don't know.
FIRST OLD WOMAN:
You're not convinced? Where's your husband?

(YERMA *shows signs of exhaustion, that of a person overcome with obsession.*)

YERMA: He's over there.

FIRST OLD WOMAN: What is he doing?

YERMA: Drinking. (*She pauses, then raises her hands to her forehead.*) Ai!

FIRST OLD WOMAN: "Ai!" "Ai!" Less "Ai!" and more spirit! I couldn't tell you anything before, but now I can.

YERMA: What are you going to tell me that I don't already know?

FIRST OLD WOMAN: Something that can't be kept quiet any more. Something they are shouting from the rooftops! It's your husband's fault! Do you hear? They can cut off my hands! Neither his father, nor his grandfather, nor his great-grandfather, behaved like a breed of real men. Heaven and earth had to come together for them to have a son! They're put together with spit! Not like your people. You have brothers and cousins for a hundred miles around! See what a curse has befallen your beauty!

YERMA: A curse! A pool of poison over the stalks of wheat!

FIRST OLD WOMAN: But you have feet: you can walk out of your house!

YERMA: Walk out?

FIRST OLD WOMAN: When I saw you at the pilgrimage, my heart turned over! Women come here to find other men. And the Saint performs the miracle! My son is sitting behind the shrine waiting for you. My house needs a woman! Go with him and the three of us will live together. My son has good blood in his veins! Like me! If you come into my house, it still has the smell of cradles! The ashes of your wedding sheets will become bread and salt for your children. Go on! Don't worry about people. And as for your husband, there are such brave hearts and sharp teeth in my house that he wouldn't dare to cross the street!

YERMA: Be quiet, be quiet, it's not that! I'd never do that! I can't go out looking. Do you think that I could have another man? What about my honor? You can't turn back the tide or have a full moon come out at midday! Go away! I'll continue on the road I have chosen. Did you really think that I could turn to another man? That I'm going to beg like a slave for what belongs to me? Understand what I am saying, so that you will never speak to me again! I am not looking for anyone.

FIRST OLD WOMAN: When you're thirsty, you're grateful for water.

YERMA: I'm like a parched field big enough to hold a thousand teams of oxen plowing, and what you give me is a little glass of water from the well! Mine is pain that is no longer of my flesh!

FIRST OLD WOMAN: (*loudly*) Then go on this way. It's what you want! Like a thistle in barren land—prickly, withered!

YERMA: (*loudly*) Barren, yes, I already know it! Barren! It's not necessary to rub my mouth with it! Don't amuse yourself like a child torturing a small animal. Ever since I got married, I've been turning that word over in my mind, but it's the first time I've heard it, the first time it's been said to my face! The first time I know that it's true!

FIRST OLD WOMAN: I have no pity for you, none! I will look for another woman for my son!

(*She goes. A large* CHORUS *of pilgrims is singing in the distance.* YERMA *goes toward the cart, and her husband appears from behind it.*)

YERMA: You were there?

JUAN: I was.

YERMA: Listening?

JUAN: Listening.

YERMA: And you heard?

JUAN: Yes.

YERMA: What of it! Leave me alone and go join the singers! (*She sits down in the tent.*)

JUAN: It's also time for me to speak.

YERMA: Speak!

JUAN: And complain.

YERMA: About what?

JUAN: I have a bitterness in my throat.

YERMA: And I, in my bones!

JUAN: I can no longer put up with this constant grieving over obscure things, unreal, things made of thin air.

YERMA: Unreal, you call it? Thin air, you call it?

JUAN: Over things that have not happened and that neither you nor I can control.

YERMA: *(violently)* Go on! Go on!

JUAN: Over things I don't care about! Do you hear? That I don't care about! I finally have to tell you! All I care about is what I can hold in my hands. What I can see with my eyes!

YERMA: *(falling to her knees in desperation)* That's it, that's it! That's what I wanted to hear from your lips! You can't see the truth when it's inside you, but how huge it is, and how it screams, when it comes out and raises its arms! You don't care! At last I have heard it!

JUAN: *(coming near her)* Tell yourself it had to turn out this way. Listen to me! *(He puts his arms around her to lift her to her feet.)* Many women would be happy living the life you do. Life is sweeter without children! I'm happy not having them. We're not to blame in any way!

YERMA: Then what were you looking for in me?

JUAN: You yourself!

YERMA: *(with excitement)* That's it! You were looking for a house, peace and quiet, and a wife! But nothing more. Is it true, what I'm saying?

JUAN: It's true! Like everyone.

YERMA: What about the rest? What about your son?

JUAN: *(fiercely)* Didn't you hear that I don't care? Don't ask me any more! I'll have to shout it in your ear for you to understand! Now let's see if once and for all you can live in peace!

YERMA: And you never considered having a son when you saw how much I wanted one?
JUAN: Never!

(They are both on the ground.)

YERMA: And I have no hope?
JUAN: No.
YERMA: Nor you?
JUAN: Nor me either. Accept it!
YERMA: Barren!
JUAN: And we shall live in peace. Both of us, quietly, with pleasure. Embrace me! *(He embraces her.)*
YERMA: What are you after?
JUAN: *You* are what I'm after! In the moonlight, you are beautiful!
YERMA: You pursue me as if I were a dove you want to devour!
JUAN: Kiss me—like this!
YERMA: I'll never do that!

(YERMA cries out and clutches her husband by the throat. He falls back. She strangles him. The CHORUS is singing.)

YERMA: Barren! Barren, but sure! Now I know it for certain! And alone! *(She stands up. People begin to gather.)* I will sleep without suddenly awakening to see if my blood is proclaiming another new blood. With my body wasted forever. What do you want to know? Don't come near me, for I have killed my son! I myself have killed my son!

(Upstage, a group gathers. The CHORUS is singing.)

CURTAIN

THE
HOUSE OF
BERNARDA ALBA

THE HOUSE OF BERNARDA ALBA

∽∽∽

Cast of Characters

MAID
LA PONCIA
BEGGAR WOMAN
BERNARDA
FIRST WOMAN
GIRL
SECOND WOMAN
THIRD WOMAN
ANGUSTIAS

THIRD WOMAN
FOURTH WOMAN
AMELIA
ADELA
MARTIRIO
MAGDALENA
MARIA JOSEFA
PRUDENCIA

ACT I

∽∽∽

A very white room in BERNARDA's *house. Thick walls. Arched doorways with jute curtains trimmed with silk tassels and ruffles. Wicker chairs. Pictures of nymphs or legendary kings in improbable landscapes. It is summer. A great, brooding silence envelopes the stage. When the curtain rises, the stage is empty. Church bells are tolling. The* MAID *enters.*

MAID: Now those bells are tolling inside my head.

LA PONCIA: *(entering, eating bread and sausage)* They've been mumbling away for over two hours now. Priests have come from every town. The church looks beautiful! Magdalena fainted during the first response.

MAID: She's the one who keeps to herself the most.

LA PONCIA: She was the only one who loved her father. Oh, thank God we're alone for a moment! I came in here to eat.

MAID: If Bernarda should see you—!

LA PONCIA: Since she's not eating, she'd like it if we all starved. Bossy tyrant! But she'll be the loser—I've opened her jar of sausages.

MAID: *(sadly, with longing)* Poncia, why don't you give me some for my little girl?

LA PONCIA: Come take a handful of garbanzos, too. Today, no one will notice.

VOICE: *(from within)* Bernarda!

137

LA PONCIA: The old lady. Is she locked up tight?

MAID: With two turns of the key.

LA PONCIA: You should fasten the bolt, too. She can pick a lock with each of her five fingers.

VOICE: Bernarda!

LA PONCIA: *(calling out)* She's coming soon! *(to the* MAID*)* Scrub everything clean. If Bernarda doesn't see things shine, she'll pull out the little hair I have left!

MAID: What a woman!

LA PONCIA: She tyrannizes everyone around her. She could sit on your heart and watch you die for a whole year without taking that cold smile off her damn face! Scrub! Scrub those tiles!

MAID: My hands are bleeding from all this scouring.

LA PONCIA: She—the most immaculate—the most decent. She—the most superior. Her poor husband has earned a good rest.

(The bells stop tolling.)

MAID: Did all their relatives come?

LA PONCIA: Hers did. His people hate her. They just came to see the body and make the sign of the cross over it.

MAID: Are there enough chairs?

LA PONCIA: More than enough. Let them sit on the floor! Since Bernarda's father died, people haven't been back to this house. She doesn't want them to see her in her domain. Damn her!

MAID: She's been good to you.

LA PONCIA: Thirty years washing her sheets. Thirty years eating her leftovers. Nights watching over her when she coughs. Entire days peering through cracks, to spy on the neighbors and bring her the gossip. A life with no secrets from each other. And yet—damn her! She should get a horrible pain—like nails piercing her eyes!

MAID: Poncia!

LA PONCIA: But I'm a good dog: I bark when I'm told to, and I snap at the beggars' heels when she sets me on them. My sons work in her fields, and they're both married now, but some day I will have had my fill.

MAID: And on that day . . . ?

LA PONCIA: On that day I'm going to lock myself in a room with her, and spit at her for a whole year! "For this, Bernarda!" *(She spits.)* "And for that!" *(She spits.)* "And for the other!" *(She spits.)* Until she's like a lizard that children have smashed to pieces. That's what she is! And so is her whole family. I certainly don't envy the way she lives. She has five girls on her hands, five ugly daughters. And except for Angustias, the oldest—who is her first husband's child and has some money—the rest? Plenty of fine lace, plenty of embroidered blouses—but bread and grapes is all they will inherit!

MAID: I would like to have what they have.

LA PONCIA: The truth is all we have is our hands and a hole in the ground when we die.

MAID: That's all the land they let us have, us who have nothing.

LA PONCIA: *(at the sideboard)* This crystal has some spots on it.

MAID: Neither soap nor flannel will get them off.

(The bells ring.)

LA PONCIA: The last prayer—I'm going over to listen. I love the way our priest sings! In the Paternoster his voice rose higher and higher—like a water pitcher being filled little by little. Of course, at the end his voice cracked, but it's glorious to hear him. Nowadays there's no one like the old sacristan Tronchapinos. He sang at the mass for my mother, may she rest in peace. The walls trembled, and when he sang the Amen, it was as if a wolf had come into the church. *(imitating him)* AME-E-EN!! *(She starts to cough.)*

MAID: You'll pulverize your windpipe!

LA PONCIA: I'd rather pulverize something else! *(She exits laughing.)*

(The MAID *scrubs. The bells ring.)*

MAID: *(imitating the bells)* Ding ding dong! Ding ding dong! May God forgive him.

BEGGAR WOMAN: *(coming in with a* LITTLE GIRL*)* Blessed be God!

MAID: Ding ding dong! Ding ding dong! May He wait many years for us! Ding ding dong!

BEGGAR WOMAN: *(loudly, with a certain irritation)* Blessed be God!

MAID: *(irritated)* Forever!

BEGGAR WOMAN: I've come for the leftovers.

(The bells stop ringing.)

MAID: You can get to the street right through that door. Today's leftovers are for me!

BEGGAR WOMAN: But you have someone who takes care of you. My daughter and I are alone!

MAID: Dogs are alone, too, and they get by.

BEGGAR WOMAN: They always give them to me.

MAID: Get out of here! Who said you could come in? Now you've tracked up my floor.

(They exit. MAID *continues scrubbing.)*

MAID: Floors polished with oil, cupboards, pedestals, steel beds. It's a bitter thing to swallow when you live in a mud hut with one plate and one spoon. I only hope that some day not one of us will be left to tell about it. *(The bells start ringing again.)* Yes, yes, clang away! Bring in the coffin with its gold trim and its fine linen cradle. In the end you will be the same as me. Rot away, Antonio Maria Benavides, stiff in your woven suit and your high boots! Rot away! Never again will you lift up my skirts behind the back gate.

(From the rear, WOMEN *in mourning begin to enter, two by two. They are wearing black skirts and carrying large handkerchiefs and black fans. They enter slowly, until they fill the stage. The* MAID *breaks into a wail.)*

MAID: Oh, Antonio Maria Benavides, you'll never again see these walls nor eat the bread of this house! Of those who served you, I loved you the most! *(She is tearing her hair.)* Must I go on living after you have gone? Must I go on living?

(As the two hundred WOMEN *finish entering,* BERNARDA ALBA *and her five* DAUGHTERS *appear.)*

BERNARDA: *(to the* MAID*)* Silence!
MAID: *(crying)* Bernarda!
BERNARDA: Less crying and more work! You should have seen to it that all of this was much cleaner to receive the mourners. Get out! This is not where you belong. *(The* MAID *leaves, crying.)* The poor are like animals; they seem to be made of other substances.
FIRST WOMAN: The poor feel their sorrow, too.
BERNARDA: But they forget it once there's a plate of garbanzos in front of them!
GIRL: *(timidly)* You must eat to live.
BERNARDA: At your age, one does not speak in front of one's elders.
FIRST WOMAN: Be quiet, child!
BERNARDA: I have never let anyone lecture me.

(They all sit. Pause.)

BERNARDA: Magdalena, don't cry! If you want to cry, crawl under the bed. Did you hear me?
SECOND WOMAN: *(to* BERNARDA*)* Have you begun to thresh the wheat?

BERNARDA: Yesterday.

THIRD WOMAN: The sun beats down like lead.

FIRST WOMAN: I haven't known it to be this hot in years.

(Pause. They all fan themselves.)

BERNARDA: Is the lemonade ready?

LA PONCIA: Yes, Bernarda. *(She enters with a large tray full of small white cups, which she passes around.)*

BERNARDA: Give some to the men.

LA PONCIA: They're already drinking on the patio.

BERNARDA: Have them leave the way they came in. I don't want them going through here.

GIRL: *(to* ANGUSTIAS*)* Pepe El Romano was with the men at the funeral.

ANGUSTIAS: He was there.

BERNARDA: His mother was there. She saw his mother. Neither she nor I saw Pepe.

GIRL: I thought I saw him.

BERNARDA: The one who *was* there was that widower from Darajalí. Standing very close to your aunt. All of us saw him.

SECOND WOMAN: *(aside, in a low voice)* Wicked! Worse than wicked!

THIRD WOMAN: *(also in a low voice)* A tongue like a knife!

BERNARDA: In church, women should look at no man but the priest, and at him only because he's wearing skirts. Whoever turns her head is on the prowl for a man.

FIRST WOMAN: *(in a low voice)* Dried up old lizard!

LA PONCIA: *(between her teeth)* Twisted by her need for a man.

BERNARDA: Blessed be God!

ALL: *(crossing themselves)* Forever blessed and holy.

BERNARDA:
Rest in peace, with the Heavenly
Host watching over you.

ALL:
Rest in peace!

BERNARDA:
> With the angel San Miguel
> And his sword of justice.

ALL:
> Rest in peace!

BERNARDA:
> With the key that opens all,
> And the hand that closes all.

ALL:
> Rest in peace!

BERNARDA:
> With all the blessed saints
> And the little lights of the fields.

ALL:
> Rest in peace!

BERNARDA:
> With our holy charity
> And the souls from land and sea.

ALL:
> Rest in peace!

BERNARDA: Grant repose to your servant Antonio Maria Benavides, and give him the crown of your sacred glory. (*She gets to her feet and sings.*) Requiem aeternum donat eis domine.

ALL: (*standing and singing in the Gregorian manner*) Et lux perpetua luceat eis. (*They cross themselves.*)

FIRST WOMAN: Good health—to pray for his soul. (*They are filing out past* BERNARDA.)

THIRD WOMAN: You'll never go without a hot loaf of bread.

SECOND WOMAN: Or shelter for your daughters.

(ANGUSTIAS *exits through the patio door.*)

FOURTH WOMAN: May you continue to reap the harvest of your marriage.

LA PONCIA: *(entering with a money bag)* The men left this bag of money for prayers.

BERNARDA: Thank them, and pour them a glass of brandy.

GIRL: *(to* MAGDALENA*)* Magdalena . . .

BERNARDA: *(to* MAGDALENA*)* Shhh! *(to the guests, who have all left)* Go home and criticize everything you've seen! I hope many years go by before you cross my threshold again.

LA PONCIA: You have nothing to complain about. The whole town came!

BERNARDA: Yes—to fill my house with the sweat of their underwear and the poison of their tongues.

AMELIA: Mother, don't talk like that!

BERNARDA: That's the way you have to talk in this damned town without a river, this town of wells! Where you always drink the water, in fear that it's poisoned!

LA PONCIA: Look what they've done to the floor!

BERNARDA: You would think a herd of goats had walked on it! (LA PONCIA *scrubs the floor.*) Adela, give me a fan.

ADELA: Here you are. *(She gives her a round fan decorated with red and green flowers.)*

BERNARDA: *(hurling the fan to the floor)* Is this the fan to give to a widow! Give me a black one, and learn to respect your father's memory.

MARTIRIO: Take mine.

BERNARDA: And you?

MARTIRIO: I don't feel warm.

BERNARDA: Well, look for another; you're going to need one. During our eight years of mourning, no wind from the street will enter this house! We'll pretend we have sealed the doors and windows with bricks. That's how it was in my father's house— and in my grandfather's house. In the meantime, you can begin to embroider your trousseaus. I have twenty bolts of cotton in the chest from which you can cut sheets and pillow cases. Magdalena can embroider them.

MAGDALENA: It's all the same to me.

ADELA: *(acidly)* If you don't want to embroider them, they'll go without embroidering. That way yours will look better!

MAGDALENA: Neither mine nor yours. I know I'm not going to get married. I'd rather carry sacks to the mill. Anything but sit in this dark room day after day!

BERNARDA: That's what it means to be a woman.

MAGDALENA: To hell with being a woman!

BERNARDA: Here, you do what I tell you to do. You can't run to your father with your stories any more. Needle and thread for females; mule and whip for males. That's how it is for people born with means.

(ADELA *exits.*)

VOICE: Bernarda! Let me out!

BERNARDA: *(in a loud voice)* Let her out now!

(*The* MAID *enters.*)

MAID: I could hardly hold her. Despite her eighty years, your mother is as strong as an oak.

BERNARDA: She takes after my grandfather. He was just the same.

MAID: Several times during the funeral, I had to cover her mouth with an empty sack because she wanted to call out to you to give her at least some dishwater to drink, and dog food. That's what she says you give her.

MARTIRIO: She's up to no good.

BERNARDA: *(to the* MAID) Let her get it off her chest in the patio.

AMELIA: She took her rings and the amethyst earrings out of her trunk. She put them on and told me she wants to get married.

(*The* DAUGHTERS *laugh.*)

BERNARDA: Go with her, and be sure she doesn't go near the well.

MAID: Don't be afraid, she won't throw herself in.

BERNARDA: It's not that—out there, the neighbors can see her from their window.

(The MAID *exits.)*

MARTIRIO: We're going to change our clothes.

BERNARDA: Very well, but don't take the shawl off your head. (ADELA *enters.)* Where is Angustias?

ADELA: *(insinuating)* I saw her peering through the cracks in the front door. The men had just left.

BERNARDA: And you, why did you go to the door, too?

ADELA: I went to see if the hens had laid.

BERNARDA: But the men must have already left.

ADELA: *(pointedly)* A group of them were still standing around outside.

BERNARDA: *(furious)* Angustias! Angustias!

ANGUSTIAS: *(entering)* What do you want?

BERNARDA: What were you looking at? And who?

ANGUSTIAS: At no one.

BERNARDA: Is it proper for a woman of your class to chase after a man on the day of her father's funeral? Answer me! Who were you looking at?

ANGUSTIAS: Me?

BERNARDA: You!

ANGUSTIAS: At no one!

BERNARDA: *(moving to her and striking her)* You weakling! You're sickening!

LA PONCIA: *(running to her)* Bernarda, calm down! *(She holds onto her.* ANGUSTIAS *is crying.)*

BERNARDA: Get out of here! All of you! *(They leave.)*

LA PONCIA: She did it without thinking what she was doing— which was clearly wrong. It bothered me to see her sneaking off toward the patio. And then she stood at the window, listening to the men's conversation and that, as usual, was not fit to be heard.

BERNARDA: That's why they come to funerals. *(curiously)* What were they talking about?

LA PONCIA: They were talking about Paca La Roseta. Last night they locked her husband up in a shed, threw her over the back of a horse, and carried her off to the top of the olive grove.

BERNARDA: And she?

LA PONCIA: She? She agreed to it. They say she rode with her breasts hanging out, and Maximiliano held onto her as if he were playing a guitar. How horrible!

BERNARDA: Then what happened?

LA PONCIA: What was bound to happen. It was dawn when they got back. Paca La Roseta had her hair undone and was wearing a crown of flowers on her head.

BERNARDA: She's the only loose woman we have in this town.

LA PONCIA: Because she's not from here. She's from far away. And the men who went with her are sons of foreigners, too. The men around here wouldn't dare do that.

BERNARDA: No. But they like to watch and talk about it, and they lick their fingers over what goes on.

LA PONCIA: They said a lot more.

BERNARDA: *(glancing nervously from side to side)* What?

LA PONCIA: I'm embarrassed to mention it.

BERNARDA: And my daughter heard them?

LA PONCIA: Of course!

BERNARDA: That one takes after her aunts. Soft and slippery— making sheep's eyes at any little barber who flatters her. How one must suffer and struggle to get people to behave decently and not like savages!

LA PONCIA: Your daughters are old enough to get married now. They give you little enough trouble. Angustias must be well over thirty by now.

BERNARDA: Thirty-nine exactly.

LA PONCIA: Imagine! And she's never had a suitor.

BERNARDA: *(furious)* Not one of them has had a suitor—or needs one! They get by very well.

LA PONCIA: I didn't mean to offend you.

BERNARDA: No one for a hundred miles around can measure up to them. The men here are not of their class. What would you have me do—turn them over to some field hand?

LA PONCIA: You should have gone to some other town.

BERNARDA: Of course—to sell them!

LA PONCIA: No, Bernarda, to trade . . . Of course, in other places, they would be the poor ones.

BERNARDA: Hold that vicious tongue!

LA PONCIA: No one can talk to you. Do we or do we not trust each other?

BERNARDA: We do not. You are my servant, and I pay you. Nothing more!

MAID: (*entering*) Don Arturo is here. He's come to discuss the will.

BERNARDA: Get busy! (*to the* MAID) You start scrubbing the patio. (*to* LA PONCIA) And you, start putting away all the clothes of the deceased in the big chest.

LA PONCIA: We could give some things away.

BERNARDA: Nothing, not one button! Not even the handkerchief we used to cover his face!

(BERNARDA *leaves slowly with a final look at the servants. Then the* MAID *exits.* AMELIA *and* MARTIRIO *enter.*)

AMELIA: Have you taken your medicine?

MARTIRIO: For all the good it's going to do me!

AMELIA: But you *have* taken it.

MARTIRIO: I do things I have no faith in, but I do them like clockwork.

AMELIA: You seem livelier since the new doctor arrived.

MARTIRIO: I feel just the same.

AMELIA: Did you notice? Adelaida wasn't at the funeral.

MARTIRIO: I knew she wouldn't be. Her fiancé won't let her go out, not even to the front gate. She used to be full of fun; now she doesn't even powder her face!

AMELIA: Nowadays, you don't know if it's better to get engaged or not.

MARTIRIO: It's all the same.

AMELIA: The problem is, we're always being criticized—they won't let us enjoy life. Adelaida must have had a terrible time.

MARTIRIO: She's afraid of Mother. She's the only one who knows the true story about her father and how he got his land. Every time she comes here, mother needles her about it. Her father killed his first wife's husband in Cuba so he could marry her himself. Then he deserted her here and ran off with another woman, who had a daughter. And then he had an affair with this girl, Adelaida's mother, and he married her after his second wife went mad and died.

AMELIA: That despicable man, why isn't he in prison?

MARTIRIO: Because men cover up this kind of thing for each other, and no one dares to make accusations.

AMELIA: But Adelaida is not to blame for that.

MARTIRIO: No. But things have a way of repeating themselves. And I see how it all follows a terrible pattern. And she'll suffer the same fate as her mother and her grandmother—the two wives of the man who fathered her.

AMELIA: What an awful thing!

MARTIRIO: It's better never to lay eyes on a man. Since I was a child, I've been afraid of them. I used to see them in the corral, harnessing the oxen and loading the sacks of wheat, with loud voices and clumsy feet, and I was always afraid of growing up, for fear of suddenly finding myself in their clutches. God made me weak and ugly and definitely set them apart from me.

AMELIA: Don't say that! Enrique Humanas was after you and he used to like you.

MARTIRIO: The things people make up! Once I stood at the window in my nightgown until daylight because his field hand's daughter told me he was going to come, and he didn't. It was all just talk. Then he married someone with more money than me.

AMELIA: And ugly as the devil.

MARTIRIO: What do they care about ugliness? All they care about is land, oxen, and a submissive bitch to cook for them.

(AMELIA *sighs*. MAGDALENA *enters*.)

MAGDALENA: What are you doing?

MARTIRIO: I'm just here.

AMELIA: And you?

MAGDALENA: I've been going through the rooms. To walk a little. To see the pictures Grandmother embroidered on canvas, the little wool dog, the black man wrestling with the lion that we liked so much when we were children. Those were happier times! A wedding lasted ten days, and wagging tongues were not in fashion. Today there's more finesse, brides wear white veils just like in the big cities, and we drink bottled wine. But we rot away inside over what people will say.

MARTIRIO: God knows what went on then!

AMELIA: *(to* MAGDALENA*)* One of your shoelaces is untied.

MAGDALENA: What difference does it make!

AMELIA: You'll step on it, and you'll fall.

MAGDALENA: One less.

MARTIRIO: Where's Adela?

MAGDALENA: Ah! She put on the green dress she made to wear on her birthday, she went out to the chicken yard, and she began to shout, "Chickens! Chickens, look at me!" I had to laugh.

AMELIA: If Mother had seen her!

MAGDALENA: Poor little thing! She's the youngest of us and she has dreams. I would give anything to see her happy.

(*There is a pause.* ANGUSTIAS *crosses the stage carrying some towels.*)

ANGUSTIAS: What time is it?

MAGDALENA: It must be twelve by now.

ANGUSTIAS: So late?

AMELIA: It's just about to strike.

(ANGUSTIAS *exits.*)

MAGDALENA: *(knowingly)* Do you know about it yet? *(indicating* ANGUSTIAS)

AMELIA: No.

MAGDALENA: Go on!

MARTIRIO: I don't know what you're referring to.

MAGDALENA: You two know more about it than I do. With your heads always together like two little sheep, but never confiding in anyone else. About Pepe El Romano.

MARTIRIO: Ah!

MAGDALENA: *(mimicking her)* Ah! They are already talking about it in town. Pepe El Romano wants to marry Angustias. He was circling the house last night, and I think he'll send someone to ask for her hand soon.

MARTIRIO: I'm glad. He's good-looking.

AMELIA: Me, too. Angustias has good qualities.

MAGDALENA: Neither one of you is glad!

MARTIRIO: Magdalena! Really!

MAGDALENA: If he wanted Angustias for herself, Angustias as a woman, I would be glad. But he wants her money. Even though Angustias is our sister, here in the family we know she's old, in poor health, and has always had the least to offer of any of us. If she looked like a dressed-up stick when she was twenty, what can she look like now that she's forty?

MARTIRIO: Don't talk that way. Luck comes to the one who least expects it.

AMELIA: After all, she is telling the truth! Angustias has all her father's money. She is the only rich one in the house. That's why, now that our father is dead and the estate is being settled, he comes for her.

MAGDALENA: Pepe El Romano is twenty-five years old, and the

best-looking man around. It would be natural for him to be interested in you, Amelia, or in our Adela, who is twenty years old, but not to come looking for the gloomiest person in this house—a woman who talks through her nose like her father did!

MARTIRIO: Maybe he likes that!

MAGDALENA: I never could stand your hypocrisy!

MARTIRIO: God forgive me!

(ADELA *enters.*)

MAGDALENA: Have the chickens seen you yet?

ADELA: What would you like me to do?

AMELIA: If Mother sees you, she'll drag you out by the hair.

ADELA: I had such dreams about this dress. I planned to wear it the day we were going out to eat watermelons at the well. There wouldn't be another like it.

MARTIRIO: It's a lovely dress.

ADELA: And it suits me very well. It's the best Magdalena has ever made.

MAGDALENA: What did the chickens say?

ADELA: They presented me with a few fleas that bit my legs.

MARTIRIO: What you could do is dye it black.

MAGDALENA: The best thing you could do is give it to Angustias to wear when she marries Pepe El Romano.

ADELA: But Pepe El Romano . . . !

AMELIA: Haven't you heard?

ADELA: No.

MAGDALENA: Well, now you know!

ADELA: But that's not possible!

MAGDALENA: Money makes everything possible!

ADELA: Is that why she went out after the funeral and was looking through the door? (*She pauses.*) And that man is capable of . . .

MAGDALENA: He's capable of anything.

(*There is a pause.*)

MARTIRIO: What are you thinking, Adela?

ADELA: I'm thinking that this period of mourning has caught me at the worst possible time.

MAGDALENA: You'll soon get used to it.

ADELA: *(bursting into tears)* I will not get used to it! I can't be locked up! I don't want my body to dry up like yours. I don't want to waste away in these rooms. Tomorrow, I'll put on my green dress and go walking down the street. I want to get out!

(The MAID enters.)

MAGDALENA: *(with authority)* Adela!

MAID: The poor thing! How she misses her father . . . *(She exits.)*

MARTIRIO: Be quiet!

AMELIA: What goes for one, goes for all!

(ADELA calms down.)

MAGDALENA: The maid almost heard you.

(The MAID enters.)

MAID: Pepe El Romano is coming down the street.

MAGDALENA: Let's go watch!

(AMELIA, MARTIRIO, and MAGDALENA run off quickly.)

MAID: *(to ADELA)* You're not going?

ADELA: I don't care.

MAID: Since he'll be coming around the corner, you can see him better from the window in your room.

(The MAID exits. ADELA hesitates for a moment, then she, too, rushes off toward her room. BERNARDA and LA PONCIA enter.)

BERNARDA: That damned will!

LA PONCIA: What a lot of money was left to Angustias!

BERNARDA: Yes.

LA PONCIA: And to the others, so much less!

BERNARDA: You've said that to me three times now, and I didn't choose to answer you. So much less, a lot less—don't remind me of it again!

(ANGUSTIAS *enters. Her face is heavily powdered.*)

BERNARDA: Angustias!

ANGUSTIAS: Mother.

BERNARDA: Have you dared to powder your face? Have you dared to even *wash* your face, on the day of your father's death?

ANGUSTIAS: He was not my father! Mine died some time ago. Don't you don't remember that?

BERNARDA: You owe more to that man, the father of your sisters, than you do to your own. Thanks to that man, your future is assured.

ANGUSTIAS: We'll see about that!

BERNARDA: If only out of decency. Out of respect!

ANGUSTIAS: Mother, let me go!

BERNARDA: Go? After you've taken that powder off your face! Weakling! Hussy! You're the image of your aunts! *(Furiously, she removes the powder from* ANGUSTIAS's *face with a handkerchief.)* Now, get out!

LA PONCIA: Bernarda, don't be so hard on her!

BERNARDA: My mother may have gone mad, but I am in control of my five senses. I know exactly what I'm doing.

(*The other* DAUGHTERS *enter.*)

MAGDALENA: What's going on?

BERNARDA: Nothing is going on.

MAGDALENA: *(to* ANGUSTIAS*)* If you're arguing about the inheritance—you're the richest, you keep it all.

ANGUSTIAS: Keep your tongue where it belongs.

BERNARDA: *(rapping the floor with her cane)* Don't entertain the illusion that you're going to control me! Until I leave this house feet first, I will make the decisions—my own, and yours!

(We hear voices offstage and MARIA JOSEFA *enters, followed by the* MAID; BERNARDA's *mother is a very old woman, decked out with flowers on her head and at her breast.)*

MARIA JOSEFA: Bernarda, where is my mantilla? I don't want any of you to have anything of mine. Not my rings nor my black moire dress. Because none of you is going to get married. Not one! Bernarda, give me my pearl necklace!

BERNARDA: *(to the* MAID) Why did you let her in?

MAID: *(trembling)* She got away from me!

MARIA JOSEFA: I escaped because I want to get married, because I want to get married to a beautiful man from the edge of the sea. Since the men around here run away from women.

BERNARDA: Be quiet, Mother!

MARIA JOSEFA: No, I won't be quiet! I don't want to see these old maids, itching to get married, with their hearts turning to dust. I want to go back to my own village. Bernarda, I want a man so I can get married and be happy.

BERNARDA: Lock her up!

MARIA JOSEFA: Let me go, Bernarda!

(The MAID *takes hold of* MARIA JOSEFA.)*

BERNARDA: Help her! All of you!

(They all drag the old woman off the stage.)

MARIA JOSEFA: I want to get away from here! Bernarda! To get married at the edge of the sea, at the edge of the sea!

CURTAIN

END OF ACT I

ACT II

〜〜〜

A white room in BERNARDA's *house. The doors at the left lead to the bedroom.* BERNARDA's DAUGHTERS *are seated in low chairs, sewing.* MAGDALENA *is embroidering.* LA PONCIA *is with them.*

ANGUSTIAS: I've already cut the third sheet.

MARTIRIO: It's for Amelia.

MAGDALENA: Angustias, shall I put Pepe's initials on it, too?

ANGUSTIAS: *(dryly)* No.

MAGDALENA: *(calling out)* Adela, aren't you coming?

AMELIA: She's must be lying down.

LA PONCIA: Something's wrong with that girl. She seems restless, shaky, frightened—as if she had a lizard between her breasts!

MARTIRIO: There's nothing more nor less wrong with her than with any of us.

MAGDALENA: All of us except Angustias!

ANGUSTIAS: I feel just fine. And anyone who doesn't like it can go to the devil!

MAGDALENA: Of course, one must admit the best things about you have always been your figure and your refinement.

ANGUSTIAS: Fortunately, I'll soon be getting out of this hell!

MAGDALENA: Perhaps you won't be getting out.

MARTIRIO: Stop that talk!

ANGUSTIAS: And besides, gold in your purse is worth more than dark eyes in your face.

156

MAGDALENA: In one ear and out the other.

AMELIA: (to LA PONCIA) Open the patio door to see if we can get a little fresh air.

MARTIRIO: Last night it was so hot I couldn't sleep.

AMELIA: Neither could I.

MAGDALENA: I got up to cool off. There was a black storm cloud and even a few drops of rain.

LA PONCIA: It was one o'clock in the morning, and the heat was rising out of the ground! I got up, too. Angustias was still at her window with Pepe.

MAGDALENA: (ironically) So late? What time did he leave?

ANGUSTIAS: Magdalena, why ask if you saw him?

AMELIA: He must have left about half-past one.

ANGUSTIAS: Yes? How do you know?

AMELIA: I heard him cough, and I heard the horse's hooves.

LA PONCIA: But I heard him leave around four o'clock.

ANGUSTIAS: That couldn't have been him.

LA PONCIA: I'm sure of it.

AMELIA: I thought so, too.

MAGDALENA: How very strange.

(There is a pause.)

LA PONCIA: Tell me, Angustias—what did he say to you, the first time he came to your window?

ANGUSTIAS: Nothing. What would he say to me? It was just talk.

MARTIRIO: It really is strange that two people who don't know each other suddenly see each other through a barred window, and just like that, they are engaged.

ANGUSTIAS: Well, it didn't bother me.

AMELIA: I'd feel—I don't know what.

ANGUSTIAS: Not me, because when a man approaches a barred window, he already knows—from people who come and go, who fetch and carry—that the answer will be yes.

MARTIRIO: Yes. But he must have asked.

ANGUSTIAS: Of course!

AMELIA: And how did he ask you?

ANGUSTIAS: No special way—"You already know why I'm here. I need a good woman, well-behaved, and that's you, if you agree."

AMELIA: These things embarass me!

ANGUSTIAS: And me, but you have to get through them.

LA PONCIA: Did he say any more?

ANGUSTIAS: Yes, he did all the talking.

MARTIRIO: What about you?

ANGUSTIAS: I couldn't. My heart almost jumped out of my mouth! It was the first time I was ever alone with a man at night.

MAGDALENA: And such a good-looking man!

ANGUSTIAS: He's not bad.

LA PONCIA: Some things are easy for people with a little experience, who talk and say things and move their hands. The first time that my husband, Evaristo El Colin, came to my window—ha, ha, ha!

AMELIA: What happened?

LA PONCIA: It was very dark. I saw him coming closer, and when he arrived, he said to me, "Good evening." "Good evening," I said to him, and we kept quiet for more than half an hour. The sweat was running down my whole body. Then Evaristo came closer and closer, as if he wanted to squeeze through the bars, and he said in a very low voice: "Come here, so I can feel you!"

(They all laugh. AMELIA *jumps up and peers out a door.)*

AMELIA: Oh! I thought Mother was coming.

MAGDALENA: She would have set us straight!

(They go on laughing.)

AMELIA: Sh-h-h-h . . . ! They'll hear us!

LA PONCIA: Afterwards, he behaved himself. Instead of taking up with another woman, he took up breeding canaries—until he died. Anyway, it's best for women like you who aren't married to know that fifteen days after the wedding, a man leaves the bed for the table, then the table for the tavern. And any woman who doesn't accept it rots away crying in a corner!

AMELIA: You went along with it.

LA PONCIA: I could handle him!

MARTIRIO: Is it true that you hit him, sometimes?

LA PONCIA: Yes, and I almost put his eye out!

MAGDALENA: That's how all women should be!

LA PONCIA: I come from the same school as your mother. One day he said something or other to me, and I killed all his canaries with a hammer!

(They laugh.)

MAGDALENA: Adela, you shouldn't miss this!

AMELIA: Adela!

(A pause.)

MAGDALENA: I'll go and see. *(She exits.)*

LA PONCIA: That child is ill.

MARTIRIO: Of course. She hardly sleeps!

LA PONCIA: What does she do?

MARTIRIO: How do I know what she does!

LA PONCIA: You would know better than me, since you sleep with only a wall between you.

ANGUSTIAS: Envy is eating her up.

AMELIA: Don't exaggerate.

ANGUSTIAS: I see it in her eyes. She's getting a look of insanity.

MARTIRIO: Don't talk about insanity. This is the last place you can say that word!

(MAGDALENA enters with ADELA.)

MAGDALENA: Well—weren't you asleep?

ADELA: My whole body aches.

MARTIRIO: *(insinuating)* Didn't you sleep well last night?

ADELA: Yes.

MARTIRIO: Well, then?

ADELA: *(forcefully)* Leave me alone! Asleep or awake, it's none of your business. I'll do what I want with my body.

MARTIRIO: It's only my concern for you.

ADELA: Concern? Or curiosity? Weren't you all sewing? Well, go on! I wish I were invisible, so I could walk through these rooms without being asked where I am going!

(The MAID enters.)

MAID: Bernarda is calling you. The man who sells lace is here.

(MAID exits. As MARTIRIO leaves, she stares fixedly at ADELA.)

ADELA: Don't look at me any more! If you want, I'll give you my eyes—they are brighter—and my back, to heal the crooked one you have. But turn your head away when I pass.

(MARTIRIO exits.)

LA PONCIA: She *is* your sister. Besides, she's the one who loves you the most.

ADELA: She follows me everywhere. Sometimes she peeks into my room to see if I'm asleep. She won't let me breathe! And it's always "What a shame about that face!" "What a shame about that body which will never belong to anyone!" No! My body will be for anyone I please.

LA PONCIA: *(pointedly, confidentially)* For Pepe El Romano. Isn't that it?

ADELA: *(taken aback)* What are you saying?

LA PONCIA: What I said, Adela.

ADELA: Be quiet!

LA PONCIA: *(loudly)* Do you think I haven't noticed?

ADELA: Lower your voice!

LA PONCIA: Do away with those thoughts!

ADELA: What do you know?

LA PONCIA: Old women can see right through the walls. Where do you go at night when you get up?

ADELA: I wish you were blind!

LA PONCIA: I have eyes in my head and my hands, when it comes to things like this. No matter how much I think about it, I can't figure out what you have in mind. Why were you standing at the open window half-naked with the light burning—the second time Pepe came to talk with your sister?

ADELA: That's not true!

LA PONCIA: Don't be childish. Leave your sister alone; and if you want Pepe El Romano, control yourself.

(ADELA *cries.*)

Besides, who says you can't marry him? Your sister Angustias is not healthy. That one won't survive her first childbirth. She's narrow in the hips, old, and from what I know I can tell she'll die. Then Pepe will do what all widowers in this country do: he'll marry the youngest, the most beautiful—and that will be you. Live on that hope or forget him, whatever you want, but don't go against the law of God.

ADELA: Be quiet!

LA PONCIA: I won't be quiet!

ADELA: Mind your own business! Spy! Traitor!

LA PONCIA: I'll have to be your shadow.

ADELA: Instead of cleaning the house and going to bed to pray for your dead, you go sticking your nose into the affairs of men and women like an old sow, so you can slobber over them.

LA PONCIA: I keep watch! So people won't spit when they come through that door.

ADELA: What a great affection for my sister has suddenly come over you!

LA PONCIA: I'm not dedicated to any of you, but I want to live in a decent house. I don't want to be disgraced in my old age.

ADELA: Your advice is useless—it's already too late now! I wouldn't fight you—you're just a servant. I'd fight against my mother, to put out this fire that rises from my legs and mouth. What can you say about me? That I lock myself in my room and don't open the door? That I don't sleep? I'm smarter than you are. See if you can catch this wild rabbit with your hands!

LA PONCIA: Don't defy me, Adela, don't defy me. Because I can raise my voice, light the lamps and make the bells ring!

ADELA: Bring out four thousand yellow flares and set them on the walls around the house. No one can keep what has to happen from happening!

LA PONCIA: You care about him that much!

ADELA: That much! When I look into his eyes, I feel as if I am slowly drinking in his blood.

LA PONCIA: I can't listen to you.

ADELA: Well, you *will* listen to me! I was afraid of you. But now, I'm stronger than you.

(ANGUSTIAS *enters*.)

ANGUSTIAS: Always arguing!

LA PONCIA: Of course. She insists I go to the store in this heat to bring her I don't know what.

ANGUSTIAS: Did you buy me that bottle of perfume?

LA PONCIA: The most expensive. And the face powder. I put them on the table in your room.

(ANGUSTIAS *exits*.)

ADELA: And hold your tongue!

LA PONCIA: We'll see about that!

(MARTIRIO, AMELIA, *and* MAGDALENA *enter*. MARTIRIO *carries some lace*.)

MAGDALENA: *(to* ADELA*)* Have you seen the lace?

AMELIA: The lace for Angustias, for her wedding sheets, is beautiful.

ADELA: *(to* MARTIRIO*)* And this?

MARTIRIO: It's for me. For a shift.

ADELA: *(sarcastically)* You have to have a sense of humor.

MARTIRIO: *(pointedly)* Just for me to see. I have no need to exhibit myself to anyone.

LA PONCIA: No one sees you in your shift.

MARTIRIO: *(pointedly, looking at* ADELA*)* Some times! But I adore undergarments! If I were rich, mine would be made of Dutch linen. It's one of the few pleasures I have left.

LA PONCIA: This lace is lovely for baby bonnets and for christening gowns. I was never able to use it on mine. Now we'll see if Angustias uses it on hers. If she decides to have babies, you'll all be sewing morning and night!

MAGDALENA: I don't plan to sew a stitch!

AMELIA: And much less raise someone else's children! Look at the women down the street, sacrificing their lives for four idiots.

LA PONCIA: They're better off than you. At least they laugh over there and you can hear them bashing each other around.

MARTIRIO: Then go to work for *them*!

LA PONCIA: No. I'm stuck in this convent now.

(There is a jingling of bells in the distance.)

MAGDALENA: It's the men coming back from work.

LA PONCIA: A minute ago it struck three!

MARTIRIO: With this sun!

ADELA: *(sitting down)* Oh, if only I could only go out to the fields, too!

MAGDALENA: *(sitting down)* We each do what we must.

MARTIRIO: *(sitting down)* That's how it is.

AMELIA: *(sitting down)(She sighs.)*

LA PONCIA: There's no greater joy than being in the fields at this time of year! Yesterday morning the harvesters arrived. Forty or fifty good-looking young men.

MAGDALENA: Where are they from this year?

LA PONCIA: From very far away. They came from the mountains. Full of spirit! Like flaming trees. Shouting and tossing stones! Last night, a woman dressed in sequins arrived in town, and she danced to the accordion, and fifteen of them arranged to take her into the olive grove. I saw them from a distance. The one who made the arrangements was a boy with green eyes, tight as a sheaf of wheat.

AMELIA: Is that true?

ADELA: It could be!

LA PONCIA: Years ago, another one of these women came, and I myself gave money to my oldest son so he could go. Men need these things.

ADELA: They are forgiven everything!

AMELIA: Being born a woman is the worst punishment.

MAGDALENA: And not even our eyes belong to us.

(There is singing in the distance, coming closer.)

LA PONCIA: It's them. They have some lovely songs.

AMELIA: They're going out to harvest now.

(Offstage, tambourines and carranacas play. There is a pause in the conversation; everyone listens in the sunstruck silence.)

CHORUS: *(offstage)*
Harvesters going to reap the wheat,
Going in search of the golden grain.
Reaping the hearts of the girls they meet
Hearts they will harvest again.

AMELIA: And they don't mind this sun!

MARTIRIO: They harvest right through the blazing heat.

ADELA: I'd like to be a harvester, so I could come and go. Then I could forget what's eating away at us.

MARTIRIO: What do *you* have to forget?

ADELA: Each of us has something.

MARTIRIO: *(profoundly)* Each of us!

LA PONCIA: Quiet! Quiet!

CHORUS: *(at a distance)*
Open your doors and your windows,
Ladies who live in this pueblo.
Harvesters beg for your roses,
Roses to trim their sombreros.

LA PONCIA: What a song!

MARTIRIO: *(nostalgically)*
Open your doors and your windows,
Ladies who live in this pueblo.

ADELA: *(passionately)*
Harvesters beg for your roses,
Roses to trim their sombreros.

(The singing fades in the distance.)

LA PONCIA: Now they're turning the corner.

ADELA: Let's go and watch them from the window in my room!

LA PONCIA: Be careful not to open it too wide—they're apt to give
it a push to see who is looking.

*(ADELA, MAGDALENA, and LA PONCIA leave. MARTIRIO stays
seated in her chair with her head in her hands.)*

AMELIA: *(going to her)* What's the matter with you?

MARTIRIO: The heat makes me ill.

AMELIA: It's nothing more than that?

MARTIRIO: I wish November would come: the rainy days, the
frost—anything but this interminable summer!

AMELIA: It soon will pass—and come again.

MARTIRIO: Of course. *(She pauses.)* What time did you fall asleep
last night?

AMELIA: I don't know. I sleep like a log. Why?

MARTIRIO: No reason, except I thought I heard people in the patio.

AMELIA: Yes?

MARTIRIO: Very late.

AMELIA: And you weren't afraid?

MARTIRIO: No. I've heard it before, other nights.

AMELIA: We should be careful. Could it have been the field hands?

MARTIRIO: The field hands come at six.

AMELIA: Perhaps a stray little mule.

MARTIRIO: *(between her teeth, with a double meaning)* That's it, that's it! A stray mule.

AMELIA: We have to warn the others.

MARTIRIO: No. No! Don't say anything! It could be I imagined it.

AMELIA: Perhaps.

(A pause. AMELIA starts to exit.)

MARTIRIO: Amelia.

AMELIA: *(in the doorway)* What?

(There is a pause.)

MARTIRIO: Nothing.

(A pause.)

AMELIA: Why did you call me?

(A pause.)

MARTIRIO: It slipped out. I didn't mean to.

(A pause.)

AMELIA: Lie down for a while.

ANGUSTIAS: *(entering, in a rage in great contrast to the preceding silences)* Where is the picture of Pepe I had under my pillow? Which of you has it?

MARTIRIO: Neither one of us.

AMELIA: It's not as if Pepe were a silver Saint Bartholomew.

ANGUSTIAS: Where is the picture?

(LA PONCIA, MAGDALENA, *and* ADELA *enter.*)

ADELA: What picture?

ANGUSTIAS: One of you has hidden it from me!

MAGDALENA: You have the effrontery to say that?

ANGUSTIAS: It was in my room, and now it's not!

MARTIRIO: Couldn't he have slipped out to the yard in the middle of the night? Pepe likes to walk around in the moonlight.

ANGUSTIAS: Don't play tricks on me! When he comes, I'm going to tell him!

LA PONCIA: Don't do that; it will turn up. *(looking at* ADELA*)*

ANGUSTIAS: I would like to know which of you has it!

ADELA: *(looking at* MARTIRIO*)* Somebody! Everybody but me!

MARTIRIO: *(meaningfully)* Of course!

BERNARDA: *(entering)* What is all this commotion in my house— and in the silence of this heavy heat? The neighbors must have their ears glued to the walls!

ANGUSTIAS: They've stolen my fiancé's picture!

BERNARDA: *(fiercely)* Who? Who?

ANGUSTIAS: Them!

BERNARDA: Which of you? *(Silence)* Answer me! *(Silence. Then to* LA PONCIA*)* Search the rooms, look in the beds! This comes from giving you too much freedom! But I will haunt your dreams! *(to* ANGUSTIAS*)* Are you sure?

ANGUSTIAS: Yes.

BERNARDA: Have you looked for it carefully?

ANGUSTIAS: Yes, Mother.

(They are all standing in an embarrassed silence.)

BERNARDA: At the end of my life, you make me drink the bitter-est poison a mother can swallow! *(calling out to* LA PONCIA*)* Can't you find it?

LA PONCIA: *(entering)* Here it is.

BERNARDA: Where did you find it?

LA PONCIA: It was . . .

BERNARDA: Don't be afraid to tell me.

LA PONCIA: *(Surprised)* Between the sheets of Martirio's bed!

BERNARDA: Is that true?

MARTIRIO: It's true.

BERNARDA: *(coming at her and hitting her)* May God strike you dead, you worthless insect! Troublemaker!

MARTIRIO: *(fiercely)* Don't you hit me, Mother!

BERNARDA: As much as I want!

MARTIRIO: If I let you! Do you hear that? Get away!

LA PONCIA: Don't be disrespectful to your mother!

ANGUSTIAS: *(seizing* BERNARDA*)* Leave her alone! Please!

BERNARDA: There aren't even tears left in those eyes!

MARTIRIO: I'm not going to cry just to please you!

BERNARDA: Why did you take the picture?

MARTIRIO: Can't I play a joke on my own sister? Why would I want it?

ADELA: It was not a joke—you've never liked playing games, never! It was something else, exploding in your heart, wanting to come out! Admit it openly, once and for all!

MARTIRIO: Be quiet, don't make me talk! Because if I talk, the walls will collapse in shame!

ADELA: A vicious tongue never stops lying!

BERNARDA: Adela!

MAGDALENA: You are both crazy!

AMELIA: And you torture us with your sinful thoughts!

MARTIRIO: Others do things that are more sinful!

ADELA: And finally even strip themselves naked, and let the river take them!

BERNARDA: Shameless!

ANGUSTIAS: It's not my fault that Pepe El Romano has chosen me!

ADELA: For your money!

ANGUSTIAS: Mother!

BERNARDA: Silence!

MARTIRIO: For your meadows and your orchards.

MAGDALENA: That's the truth!

BERNARDA: Silence, I said! I saw the storm coming, but I didn't think it would burst so soon. Oh, what a hailstone of hate you have thrown on my heart! But I'm not old yet, and I have five chains for you, and this house my father built so not even the weeds will know of my desolation. Get out of here!

(They leave. BERNARDA sits down desolate. LA PONCIA is standing close to the wall. BERNARDA collects herself and strikes the floor with her cane.)

BERNARDA: I must use a firm hand with them. Bernarda: Remember, this is your duty!

LA PONCIA: May I speak?

BERNARDA: Speak. I'm sorry you heard. It's never wise to let an outsider into the family circle.

LA PONCIA: What I have seen, I have seen.

BERNARDA: Angustias must get married right away.

LA PONCIA: Of course. We have to get her away from here.

BERNARDA: Not her. Him!

LA PONCIA: Of course. We must get him far away from here. Good thinking!

BERNARDA: I don't think. There are things we cannot, and should not, *think*! I give orders.

LA PONCIA: And do you believe he'll want to leave?

BERNARDA: What's going on in that head of yours?

LA PONCIA: He—of course—will marry Angustias.

BERNARDA: Go on! I know you well enough to see you already have your knife out.

LA PONCIA: I never thought giving a warning would be called murder.

BERNARDA: You have something to warn me about?

LA PONCIA: I'm not making accusations, Bernarda. I'm only telling you: open your eyes and you'll see.

BERNARDA: See what?

LA PONCIA: You've always been clever. You've seen evil in people from a hundred miles away. I have often believed you could read people's minds. But your children are your children. And about them, you are blind.

BERNARDA: Are you referring to Martirio?

LA PONCIA: Well, when it comes to Martirio . . . *(with curiosity)* Why would she hide the picture?

BERNARDA: After all, she says it was a joke. What else could it be?

LA PONCIA: *(deliberately)* Do you believe that?

BERNARDA: *(vigorously)* I don't *believe* it—it is so!

LA PONCIA: All right. It's your family we're dealing with. But if it were the neighbor across the street—what would you think?

BERNARDA: Now you're beginning to sharpen your knife.

LA PONCIA: Bernarda, something monstrous is happening here. I don't want to blame you, but you haven't allowed your daughters any freedom. Martirio is romantic, no matter what you say. Why didn't you let her marry Enrique Humanas? Why did you send him a message not to come to her window, the very day he was coming?

BERNARDA: And I would do it a thousand times again! My blood will never mix with the blood of the Humanas—not as long as I live. His father was a field hand.

LA PONCIA: This is what comes of putting on airs!

BERNARDA: I do because I can afford to! And you don't because you know very well what you come from.

LA PONCIA: *(with hatred)* Don't remind me of that! I'm old now. I've always been grateful for your protection.

BERNARDA: *(drawing herself up)* It wouldn't seem so!

LA PONCIA: *(with hatred masked in sweetness)* Martirio will forget about this.

BERNARDA: And if she doesn't forget about it, the worse for her! I don't think "something monstrous" is happening here. Nothing is happening here. That's what you'd like. And if something does happen someday, rest assured it will not go beyond these walls!

LA PONCIA: I don't know about that—there are also people in town who can read secret thoughts from a distance.

BERNARDA: How you'd like seeing me and my daughters on our way to the whorehouse!

LA PONCIA: No one can know her own fate.

BERNARDA: I do know my fate—and that of my daughters. We'll leave the brothel for a certain woman who is already dead.

LA PONCIA: Bernarda, respect the memory of my mother!

BERNARDA: Stop hounding me, you with your evil thoughts!

(There is a pause.)

LA PONCIA: It's best if I don't get mixed up in anything.

BERNARDA: That's what you should do: work and keep your mouth shut. It's the obligation of those who are paid to work.

LA PONCIA: But I can't. Don't you think that Pepe would be better off married to Martirio or—Yes!—to Adela?

BERNARDA: I do *not* think so.

LA PONCIA: Adela. She is El Romano's true love.

BERNARDA: Things are never the way we would like them to be.

LA PONCIA: But it's very hard for them to turn away from their true feelings. It seems wrong for Pepe to be with Angustias, to me and to other people, and even to the air. Who knows if they'll get their way!

BERNARDA: Here we go again! Your insinuations give me nightmares. And I don't want to listen to you, because if things turn out the way you say they will, I will have to scratch your face.

LA PONCIA: The blood wouldn't get as far as the river!

BERNARDA: Fortunately, my daughters respect me and have never gone against my will.

LA PONCIA: That's true. But as soon as you turn them loose, they'll be up on the roof.

BERNARDA: I'll get them down soon enough—by throwing stones at them.

LA PONCIA: Of course, you're the most valiant.

BERNARDA: I've always relished a good challenge.

LA PONCIA: But it's strange! At her age! Just look at how taken Angustias is with her fiancé! And he seems to be smitten, too! Yesterday, my oldest son told me that at half-past four in the morning when he went by with his oxen, they were still talking!

BERNARDA: At half-past four?

ANGUSTIAS: *(entering)* That's a lie!

LA PONCIA: That's what I was told.

BERNARDA: *(to* ANGUSTIAS*)* Go on!

ANGUSTIAS: For more than a week Pepe has been leaving here at one o'clock. May God strike me dead if I'm lying!

MARTIRIO: *(entering)* I heard him leave at four, too.

BERNARDA: But did you see him with your own eyes?

MARTIRIO: I didn't want to be seen. Don't you usually talk through the window on the side of the house?

ANGUSTIAS: I talk through the window in my bedroom.

(ADELA *appears at the door.*)

MARTIRIO: Then . . .

BERNARDA: What is going on here?

LA PONCIA: Careful, you'll find out! But in any case, Pepe was at one of the windows of your house at four in the morning.

BERNARDA: Do you know that for certain?

LA PONCIA: You don't know anything for certain in this life.

ADELA: Mother, don't listen to someone who wants to destroy us all!

BERNARDA: I will know how to find out. If the people in this town want to bear false witness, they will come up against my solid rock. This matter is not to be discussed. Sometimes other people stir up a wave of mud in order to destroy us.

MARTIRIO: I don't like to lie.

LA PONCIA: So something is happening.

BERNARDA: Nothing is happening. I was born with my eyes open. Now I'll be vigilant and never close them until I die.

ANGUSTIAS: I have the right to know.

BERNARDA: You have no right except to obey. No one is going to push or pull me. *(to* LA PONCIA*)* And you take care of your own affairs. Here no one will take one step without my knowing it.

MAID: *(entering)* There's a big crowd up the street! And all the neighbors are at their doors!

BERNARDA: *(to* LA PONCIA*)* Run and find out what's happening!

(The MAID *and* LA PONCIA *hurry off.* ADELA, MARTIRIO, *and* ANGUSTIAS *start to run after them.)*

BERNARDA: Where are you going? I always knew you were the sort of women who would hang out the windows and disgrace their mourning. All of you, to the patio!

(They exit first, and then BERNARDA. *We hear distant voices.* MARTIRIO *and* ADELA *enter. They stand there listening, not daring to take another step toward the outside door.)*

MARTIRIO: Be grateful I didn't happen to open my mouth.

ADELA: I could have said some things, too.

MARTIRIO: And what could you say? Wanting is not doing.

ADELA: She who can, does—and she wins. You wanted to, but you couldn't.

MARTIRIO: You won't go on like this much longer.

ADELA: I'll have it all!

MARTIRIO: I'll tear you out of his arms!

ADELA: *(pleading)* Martirio, leave me alone!

MARTIRIO: Not for either of us!

ADELA: He wants me in his house!

MARTIRIO: I saw the way he embraced you!

ADELA: I didn't want to! It was like being dragged by a rope.

MARTIRIO: I'd rather be dead!

(MAGDALENA *and* ANGUSTIAS *appear. The crowd noises grow louder.*)

LA PONCIA: (*entering with* BERNARDA) Bernarda!

BERNARDA: What is going on?

LA PONCIA: Librata's daughter, the one who's not married, just had a baby and no one knows by who.

ADELA: A baby?

LA PONCIA: And to hide her shame, she killed it and put it under some rocks. But some dogs, with more feelings than many creatures, pulled it out, and as if led by the hand of God, they put it on her doorstep. Now they want to kill her. They're dragging her through the street below, and the men are running down the paths and out of the olive groves, shouting so loud the fields are trembling.

BERNARDA: Yes! Have them all bring whips made of olive branches and ax handles! Have them all come to kill her!

ADELA: No! No! Not kill her!

MARTIRIO: Yes, let's go out there, too!

BERNARDA: Any woman who tramples on decency should pay for it!

(*Outside, a woman screams, and there is a great uproar.*)

ADELA: They should let her go! Don't go out there!

MARTIRIO: (*looking at* ADELA) She should pay her debt!

BERNARDA: (*in the archway*) Finish her before the police get here! Burning coals in the place where she sinned!

ADELA: (*clutching her womb*) No! No!

BERNARDA: Kill her! Kill her!

CURTAIN

END OF ACT II

ACT III

∽∽∽

The interior patio of BERNARDA'*s house. It is night. Four white walls washed with blue light. The decor must be one of perfect simplicity. The doors, illuminated by the light from inside, cast a delicate glow on the scene. At center, a table with an argon lamp where* BERNARDA *and her* DAUGHTERS *are eating.* LA PONCIA *is serving them.* PRUDENCIA *is seated at one side. The curtain rises on total silence, interrupted only by the clatter of dishes and table-ware.*

PRUDENCIA: I'm going now. It's been a long visit. (*She rises.*)
BERNARDA: Wait, Prudencia! We never see each other.
PRUDENCIA: Has the last call for the rosary sounded?
LA PONCIA: Not yet.

(PRUDENCIA *sits down.*)

BERNARDA: How is your husband getting on?
PRUDENCIA: The same.
BERNARDA: We don't see him, either.
PRUDENCIA: You know how he is. Ever since he fought with his
  brothers over the inheritance, he hasn't used the front door.
  He puts up a ladder, climbs over the wall, and over the corral.
BERNARDA: He's a real man! And with your daughter?
PRUDENCIA: He has not forgiven her.

175

BERNARDA: He is right.

PRUDENCIA: I don't know what to tell you. I suffer because of it.

BERNARDA: A daughter who disobeys stops being a daughter and becomes an enemy.

PRUDENCIA: I just let the water flow. The only comfort I have left is to take refuge in the church, but since my eyes are failing, I'll have to stop coming because the children tease me.

(There is a loud pounding on the wall.)

PRUDENCIA: What is that?

BERNARDA: The breeding stallion, locked up and kicking the wall. *(loudly)* Shackle him and let him out in the corral! *(confidentially)* He must be in heat.

PRUDENCIA: Are you going to breed him with your new mares?

BERNARDA: At sunrise.

PRUDENCIA: You've been wise to build up your herd.

BERNARDA: Thanks to money and a lot of unpleasantness.

LA PONCIA: *(interrupting)* But she has the best herd in this part of the country. It's too bad prices are down.

BERNARDA: Would you like some cheese and honey?

PRUDENCIA: I have no appetite.

(We hear the pounding again.)

LA PONCIA: For God's sake!

PRUDENCIA: It gave me a start!

BERNARDA: *(rising furiously)* Must I say things twice? Let him out so he can roll in the piles of straw. *(She pauses, as if listening to the hired hands.)* Well, lock the mares in the stable, but turn him loose before he kicks down the walls! *(She goes back to the table and sits.)* Oh, what a life!

PRUDENCIA: Struggling like a man.

BERNARDA: That's the way it is.

(ADELA gets up from the table.)

BERNARDA: Where are you going?

ADELA: For a drink of water.

BERNARDA: *(calling out)* Bring a pitcher of cold water! *(to* ADELA*)* You may sit down.

(ADELA *sits down.)*

PRUDENCIA: What about Angustias, when will she get married?

BERNARDA: They are coming to ask for her hand in three days.

PRUDENCIA: You must be pleased!

ANGUSTIAS: Of course!

ADELA: *(to* MAGDALENA*)* Now you've spilled the salt!

MAGDALENA: Your luck can't get any worse than it is now.

AMELIA: It's always a bad sign.

BERNARDA: That's enough!

PRUDENCIA: Has he given you the ring yet?

ANGUSTIAS: Do look at it. *(She holds it out.)*

PRUDENCIA: It's lovely. Three pearls! In my day, pearls meant tears.

ANGUSTIAS: But things have changed now.

ADELA: I don't think so. Things always mean the same. Engagement rings are supposed to be diamonds.

PRUDENCIA: It's more appropriate.

BERNARDA: With pearls or without them, things are what you make of them.

MARTIRIO: Or what God makes of them.

PRUDENCIA: Your furniture, they tell me, is lovely.

BERNARDA: I spent sixteen thousand *reales.*

LA PONCIA: *(interjecting)* The best is the clothes cupboard with mirrors.

PRUDENCIA: I never saw one of those fancy things.

BERNARDA: All we had was a chest.

PRUDENCIA: What's important is that everything goes well.

ADELA: And you never know.

BERNARDA: There's no reason why it shouldn't.

(Bells are heard, very far off.)

PRUDENCIA: The last call. *(to* ANGUSTIAS*)* I'll come back soon, so you can show me your clothes.

ANGUSTIAS: Whenever you like.

PRUDENCIA: *Good night.* God be with you.

BERNARDA: Good-bye, Prudencia.

The five DAUGHTERS together: God go with you.

(There is a pause. PRUDENCIA *leaves.)*

BERNARDA: We are through eating now.

(They get up from the table.)

ADELA: I'm going as far as the front gate to stretch my legs and get a little fresh air.

*(*MAGDALENA *sits in a low chair against the wall.)*

AMELIA: I'll go with you.

MARTIRIO: Me too.

ADELA: *(with repressed hatred)* I'm not going to get lost.

AMELIA: You should have company at night.

(They go out. BERNARDA *sits;* ANGUSTIAS *is clearing the table.)*

BERNARDA: I've already told you I want you to speak to your sister Martirio. What happened with the picture was just a joke, and you should forget it.

ANGUSTIAS: You know she doesn't like me.

BERNARDA: We each know what we're thinking inside. I don't pry into people's feelings, but I do want to keep up appearances and have harmony in the family. Do you understand that?

ANGUSTIAS: Yes.

BERNARDA: That's settled, then.

MAGDALENA: *(half asleep)* Anyway, you're going to be leaving very soon! *(She falls asleep.)*

ANGUSTIAS: Not soon enough, I feel!

BERNARDA: What time did you finish talking last night?

ANGUSTIAS: At half-past twelve.

BERNARDA: What does Pepe have to say?

ANGUSTIAS: I find him distracted. He always talks to me as if he's thinking of something else. If I ask him what's wrong, he answers: "We men have our own problems."

BERNARDA: You shouldn't ask him. And much less after you're married. Speak if he speaks, and look at him when he looks at you. That way you won't quarrel.

ANGUSTIAS: Mother, I think he hides many things from me.

BERNARDA: Don't try to find out about them. Don't ask him. And, above all, don't ever let him see you cry.

ANGUSTIAS: I should be happy, and I'm not.

BERNARDA: It's all the same.

ANGUSTIAS: I often stare very hard at Pepe until he grows blurred behind the bars of the window, as if he were being covered by a cloud of dust like the ones the sheep stir up.

BERNARDA: You're just tired.

ANGUSTIAS: I hope so.

BERNARDA: Is he coming tonight?

ANGUSTIAS: No. He went to the city with his mother.

BERNARDA: Then we'll get to bed earlier. Magdalena!

ANGUSTIAS: She's asleep.

(ADELA, MARTIRIO, *and* AMELIA *enter.*)

AMELIA: What a dark night!

ADELA: You can't see two steps ahead of you.

MARTIRIO: A good night for thieves, for someone who needs a hiding place.

ADELA: The stallion was in the middle of the corral—so white! Twice as big, completely filling the darkness!

AMELIA: It's true. It was frightening! It was like an apparition.

ADELA: There are stars in the sky as big as fists.

MARTIRIO: This one kept staring at them so much, she almost broke her neck.

ADELA: Don't you like them?

MARTIRIO: I don't care what goes on above the rooftops. I have enough with what goes on inside these rooms.

ADELA: That's how you are.

BERNARDA: She has her way and you have yours.

ANGUSTIAS: Good night.

ADELA: Are you going to bed now?

ANGUSTIAS: Yes. Pepe is not coming tonight. *(She exits.)*

ADELA: Mother, when there's a shooting star or a flash of lightning, why do we say:

Blessed Santa Barbara, why
Are you writing up so high
With holy water in the sky?

BERNARDA: The ancient people times knew many things that we've forgotten.

AMELIA: I close my eyes so I won't see them!

ADELA: Not me. I like to see things blazing through the sky, after being motionless year after year.

MARTIRIO: But these things have nothing to do with us.

BERNARDA: And it's best not to think about them.

ADELA: What a beautiful night! I'd like to stay up very late so I could enjoy the cool air from the fields.

BERNARDA: But we have to go to bed. Magdalena!

AMELIA: She dozed off.

BERNARDA: Magdalena!

MAGDALENA: *(annoyed)* Leave me in peace!

BERNARDA: Go to bed!

MAGDALENA: *(getting up peevishly)* You don't leave a person alone! *(She leaves, grumbling.)*

AMELIA: Good night. *(She goes.)*

BERNARDA: You go, too.

MARTIRIO: Why isn't Angustias's fiancé coming tonight?

BERNARDA: He went on a trip.

MARTIRIO: *(looking at* ADELA*)* Ah!

ADELA: See you in the morning. *(She leaves.* MARTIRIO *drinks some water and exits slowly, looking toward the door to the patio.)*

LA PONCIA: *(entering)* Are you still here?

BERNARDA: Enjoying this quiet time, and unable to find any trace of that "monstrous thing" you claim is happening here.

LA PONCIA: Bernarda, let's forget about that conversation.

BERNARDA: In this house there is no question of "yes" or "no." My vigilance takes care of that.

LA PONCIA: Nothing is happening on the surface, it's true. Your daughters are stuck away in a cupboard and that's how they live. But neither you nor anyone else can see into their hearts.

BERNARDA: My daughters breathe easily.

LA PONCIA: You care about that because you're their mother. For me, looking after your house is enough.

BERNARDA: Now, you've decided to become silent!

LA PONCIA: I know my place, and I'm at peace.

BERNARDA: The trouble is you have nothing to talk about. If there were grass growing in this house, you'd bring every sheep in the neighborhood in to graze.

LA PONCIA: I cover up more than you think.

BERNARDA: Does your son still see Pepe at four o'clock in the morning? Do they still tell the same malicious stories about this house?

LA PONCIA: They say nothing.

BERNARDA: Because they can't! Because there's no meat to bite into. Thanks to my watchful eyes.

LA PONCIA: Bernarda, I don't want to talk because I'm afraid of what you'll do. But don't be too sure.

BERNARDA: Absolutely sure.

LA PONCIA: When you least expect it, lightning strikes! When you least expect it, your heart stops!

BERNARDA: Nothing is happening here. I'm quite prepared to deal with your suppositions.

LA PONCIA: Well, all the better for you!

BERNARDA: All the better!

MAID: *(entering)* I have finished washing the dishes now. Is there anything else you want, Bernarda?

BERNARDA: *(getting up)* Nothing. I'm going to bed.

LA PONCIA: What time do you want me to call you?

BERNARDA: Don't. Tonight I'm going to sleep well. *(She exits.)*

LA PONCIA: When you can't fight the tide, it's easier to turn your back, so you don't see it.

MAID: She's so proud she puts a blindfold on herself.

LA PONCIA: There's nothing I can do. I tried to put a stop to all this, but now it frightens me too much. Do you hear this silence? Well, there's a storm brewing in every room. The day it bursts, we'll all be swept away! I've said what I had to say.

MAID: Bernarda thinks that no one can stand up to her. She doesn't realize the power a man can have over lonely women.

LA PONCIA: It's not all Pepe El Romano's fault. It's true that last year he was after Adela, and she was crazy for him. But she should have known her place and not led him on. A man is a man.

MAID: They say he spoke with to Adela many times.

LA PONCIA: It's true. *(lowering her voice)* Among other things.

MAID: I don't know what's going to happen here.

LA PONCIA: I'd like to cross the ocean and get away from this house of turmoil.

MAID: Bernarda is rushing the wedding day, and perhaps nothing will happen.

LA PONCIA: Things have already gone too far. Adela has made up her mind, no matter what happens; and the others keep watch, all the time.

MAID: Martirio, too?

LA PONCIA: She's the worst! She's a pit of poison! She knows El Romano is not for her, and she would crush the world if it were in her hand!

MAID: They are wicked.

LA PONCIA: They are women without men, that's all. When it

comes to that, you forget even your own blood. Shhh! *(She listens.)*

MAID: What is it?

LA PONCIA: *(stands up)* The dogs are barking.

MAID: Someone must have come through the front gate.

(ADELA enters, wearing white petticoats and a camisole.)

LA PONCIA: Didn't you go to bed?

ADELA: I'm getting a drink of water. *(She drinks from a glass on the table.)*

LA PONCIA: I thought you were asleep.

ADELA: I woke up thirsty. And what about you, aren't you going to bed?

MAID: Right now.

(ADELA exits.)

LA PONCIA: Let's go.

MAID: We've earned our sleep. Bernarda doesn't let me rest the whole day.

LA PONCIA: Bring the lamp.

MAID: The dogs are acting crazy!

LA PONCIA: They're not going to let us sleep.

(They exit. The stage is almost completely dark. MARIA JOSEFA enters, carrying a baby ewe (ovejita-aw-veh-hee-tah) in her arms.)

MARIA JOSEFA:
Ovejita, child of mine,
Come with me to the edge of the sea.
The little ant is at her door,
I'll give you my breast, and bread.

Bernarda—
Face of a leopard.

Magdalena—
Face of a hyena.
Ovejita—
Mee-ee-ee, mee-ee-ee.
Underneath the palms at the gates of Bethlehem.

You and I don't want to sleep
The door will open on its own
And you and I will hide ourselves
In a hut made of coral on the beach.

Bernarda—
Face of a leopard.
Magdalena—
Face of a hyena.
Ovejita—
Mee-ee-ee, mee-ee-ee.
Underneath the palms at the gates of Bethlehem.

(She leaves, singing.)

*(*ADELA *enters. She looks furtively from side to side and disappears through the door to the patio.* MARTIRIO *enters through another door and stands waiting in anguish at the center of the stage. She, too, is in petticoats. She's wearing a short black shawl over her shoulders.* MARIA JOSEFA *enters downstage of her.)*

MARTIRIO: Grandmother, where are you going?
MARIA JOSEFA: Are you going to open the door for me? Who are you?
MARTIRIO: How did you get here?
MARIA JOSEFA: I escaped. Who are you?
MARTIRIO: Go to bed.
MARIA JOSEFA: You're Martirio, now I see you. Martirio, face of a martyr. And when are you going to have a child? I've had this one.
MARTIRIO: Where did you catch that lamb?

MARIA JOSEFA: I know it's a lamb. But why can't a lamb be a child? It's better to have a lamb than to have nothing. Bernarda, face of a leopard; Magdalena, face of a hyena.

MARTIRIO: Don't talk so loud.

MARIA JOSEFA: It's true. Everything is very dark. Just because I have white hair you think I can't have babies. And—Yes! Babies and babies and babies! This child will have white hair, and have another child, and that one, another, and all of us with hair of snow will be like the waves, one after another after another. Then we'll all settle down, and we'll all have white hair, and we'll be foam on the sea. Why isn't there any foam here? Here there is nothing but black mourning shawls.

MARTIRIO: Quiet! Be quiet!

MARIA JOSEFA: When my neighbor had a child, I used to take chocolate to him, and then she would bring him to me, and so on—forever and ever and ever. You will have white hair, but the neighbors won't come. I have to go, but I'm afraid the dogs will bite me. Will you come with me out to the fields? I love the fields. I love houses, but houses that are open, where the women are stretched out on their beds with their little children, and the men are outside sitting in their chairs. Pepe El Romano is a giant! You all want him. But he is going to devour you, because you are grains of wheat. Not grains of wheat! Frogs without tongues!

MARTIRIO: Come on. Go to bed. (*She pushes her.*)

MARIA JOSEFA: Yes, but later you'll let me out, won't you?

MARTIRIO: Of course.

MARIA JOSEFA: (*weeping*)
Ovejita, child of mine,
Come with me to the edge of the sea.
A little ant stands at her door,
I'll give you my breast, and bread.

(MARTIRIO *locks the door through which* MARIA JOSEFA *exited, and goes toward the door to the patio. She hesitates there, then takes two more steps.*)

MARTIRIO: *(quietly)* Adela! *(She pauses, then goes closer to the door.)* *(loudly)* Adela!

(ADELA appears. Her hair is a bit mussed up.)

ADELA: Why are you looking for me?

MARTIRIO: Stay away from that man!

ADELA: Who are you to tell me that?

MARTIRIO: That's no place for a decent woman!

ADELA: How you'd love to be there yourself!

MARTIRIO: *(loudly)* The time has come for me to speak! Things can't go on like this!

ADELA: This is only the beginning. I had the strength to go forward—the looks and the courage you don't have! I saw death under this roof, and I went out to look for what is mine, what belongs to me!

MARTIRIO: That heartless man came here for some one else. You have come between them.

ADELA: He came for the money, but his eyes were always on me.

MARTIRIO: I won't allow you to snatch him away! He is going to marry Angustias.

ADELA: You know better than I that he doesn't love her.

MARTIRIO: I know.

ADELA: You know, because you've seen it, he loves me!

MARTIRIO: Yes.

ADELA: *(coming close to her)* He loves me! He loves me!

MARTIRIO: Stick a knife in me if you like, but don't say that to me again!

ADELA: That's why you're trying to keep me from going off with him. You don't care if he embraces a woman he doesn't love. Me neither. Yes, he could spend a hundred years with Angustias, but if he embraces me it seems terrible to you because you love him, too! You love him!

MARTIRIO: *(dramatically)* Yes! Let me say it openly. Yes! Let my breast explode like a bitter pomegranate! I love him!

ADELA: *(impulsively going to embrace her)* Martirio, Martirio, it's not my fault!

MARTIRIO: Don't embrace me! Don't try to soften my eyes. My blood is no longer yours! Though I try to think of you as a sister, now I see you only as a woman. *(She pushes her away.)*

ADELA: There's no solution here. If one of us has to drown, let her drown! Pepe El Romano is mine! He takes me into the reeds at the edge of the river.

MARTIRIO: Never!

ADELA: I can't stand the horror of this house any more, not after knowing the taste of his mouth. I will be what he wants me to be. With the whole town against me, branding me with their fiery fingers, persecuted by people who say they are decent, and I'll wear a crown of thorns like any mistress of a married man!

MARTIRIO: Be quiet!

ADELA: Yes! Yes! *(quietly)* We will go to sleep. We will let him marry Angustias; I don't care any more. But I'll go off by myself to a little house where he will see me when he wants, when he has the need.

MARTIRIO: That will not happen as long as I have one drop of blood in my body.

ADELA: Not just you—you're weak—I could bring a wild stallion to his knees with the strength in my little finger!

MARTIRIO: Don't raise your voice, it irritates me. My heart is filled with a force so vicious that, in spite of myself, it smothers me.

ADELA: They teach us to love our sisters. God must have abandoned me out in the middle of the darkness, because I see you as if I had never seen you before.

(A whistle is heard. ADELA *runs to the door, but* MARTIRIO *blocks it.)*

MARTIRIO: Where are you going?

ADELA: Get away from the door!

MARTIRIO: Get past if you can!
ADELA: Get away!

(They struggle.)

MARTIRIO: *(loudly)* Mother! Mother!

(BERNARDA *appears in her petticoats and a black shawl.*)

BERNARDA: Stop it! Stop it! How deprived I am with no bolt of lightning in between my fingers!
MARTIRIO: *(pointing at* ADELA*)* She was with him! Look at her petticoats, covered with straw!
BERNARDA: That is the bed of a sinful woman! *(She goes toward* ADELA, *furiously.)*
ADELA: *(confronting her)* The shouting in this prison is over. *(She seizes her mother's walking stick and breaks it in two.)* This is what I do with the tyrant's rod! Don't take one step more. No one but Pepe gives me orders.
MAGDALENA: *(entering)* Adela!

(LA PONCIA *and* ANGUSTIAS *enter.*)

ADELA: I am his woman. *(to* ANGUSTIAS*)* Get that into your head—and go out to the corral and tell him that. He will be master of this entire house! He's out there, breathing like a lion!
ANGUSTIAS: My God!
BERNARDA: The gun! Where is the gun? *(She runs out.)*

(MARTIRIO *follows.* AMELIA *appears in the background, looking on in terror, pressing her head against the wall.*)

ADELA: No one can stop me! *(She starts to leave.)*
ANGUSTIAS: *(seizing her)* You're not leaving here—you and your triumphant body! Thief! You're a dishonor to our house!

MAGDALENA: Let her go where we'll never see her again.

(A *shot is heard.*)

BERNARDA: *(entering)* I dare you to find him now!
MARTIRIO: *(entering)* That's the end of Pepe El Romano!
ADELA: Pepe! My God! Pepe! *(She runs out of the room.)*
LA PONCIA: Did you kill him?
MARTIRIO: No. He ran off on his horse.
BERNARDA: It was not my fault. A woman is not trained to use a gun.
MAGDALENA: Then why did you say that?
MARTIRIO: Because of her! I would have spilled a river of blood over her head!
LA PONCIA: Damn you!
MAGDALENA: You're a fiend!
BERNARDA: Though it's better this way. *(There is a heavy thud.)* Adela. Adela!
LA PONCIA: *(at the door)* Open up!
BERNARDA: Open up! Don't think these walls can hide your shame!
MAID: *(entering)* The neighbors are awake!
BERNARDA: *(in a low, fierce voice)* Open up, or I'll break down the door! *(She backs away from the door.)* Bring a hammer!

(LA PONCIA *shoves the door open and enters. Then, she screams and runs out.*)

BERNARDA: What is it?
LA PONCIA: *(her hands at her throat)* We should never come to that end!

(*The* SISTERS *draw back from the door. The* MAID *crosses herself.* BERNARDA *screams and steps forward.*)

LA PONCIA: Don't go in!

BERNARDA: No. Not me! Pepe; you may go running off, alive, through the shadows of the poplars, but one day you will fall. Cut her down. My daughter has died a virgin. Carry her to her room and dress her in white. No one will say a thing. She died a virgin. Send word for the bells to toll twice at dawn.

MARTIRIO: She was fortunate a thousand times over—she had him.

BERNARDA: I want no weeping. We must look at death, face to face. Silence! *(to another* DAUGHTER*)* Be quiet, I said! *(to another* DAUGHTER*)* Tears, when you're alone. We will all drown ourselves in a sea of mourning. She, the youngest daughter of Bernarda Alba, has died a virgin. Do you hear me? Silence, silence I said! Silence!

CURTAIN

TRANSLATOR'S NOTES

Carmen Zapata and I began to translate the plays of Lorca in 1977, not by choice, but of necessity. Carmen was spending her off-camera hours creating a new Los Angeles theatre company, the Bilingual Foundation of the Arts. Its artistic director, Margarita Galban, had been a *Lorquiana* since her school days in pre-Castro Havana and throughout an acting career in Mexico. *La Galban* had appeared across the length and breadth of Mexico playing Lorca's women. Now a director, she wanted to stage Lorca's plays for U.S. audiences—both Hispanic and non-Hispanic.

In order to launch BFA, Carmen was willing, once a season, to take months off from her Hollywood acting schedule. And like any actress worth her salt, she was eager to get her teeth into the extraordinary repertory of feminine roles in the Lorca canon. But there were no translations that she felt were playable. And BFA's audiences and actors—unlike some others—would not be apt to blame weak translations on the original author.

For even in its earliest days, BFA was living up to its name. On modest budgets, working in spaces donated by the film studios and community cultural centers, it rehearsed and performed bilingually—with the actors playing their roles one night in Spanish, the next night in English. And already, its growing audience was increasingly interested in seeing two performances, one in each language.

So we set to work to make a translation of *Bodas de Sangre* that would be accepted by these actors and these audiences. And I began to discover how lucky I was. To begin with, I enjoyed the partnership of a superbly trained actress whose native tongue was Spanish, but who has spent her long career playing both Anglos and *Latinas*. My own years in the theatre, producing classics and often adapting them, had taught me that dialogue is, first and last, *spoken*.

How we railed at each other—every line was whispered, shouted, chattered, screamed, chanted, even sung. We worked through a California winter of windstorms and mudslides by my fireside in Benedict Canyon and a summer of smog and drought by Carmen's poolside in Van Nuys. In July, the cast had begun Spanish-language rehearsals. Four weeks later, they were given our "final" draft, and we began to attend rehearsals in English.

What a revelation! Immersed in the original, mentally and emotionally, the actors had all sorts of problems with our translation. At this stage of rehearsals, they were thinking and feeling in Spanish, but were being asked to speak in English. When good actors just couldn't force our words out, we knew that changes were called for. Hundreds of changes, from single words to complete sentences. Occasionally, the actors themselves could tell us what was needed. More often, we had to be there at the moment when they stumbled, then talk to them during a rehearsal break, retire to the lobby to talk through our own solution, and then scribble away in our seats, rewriting, rewriting, rewriting.

The process continued after *Blood Wedding* enjoyed a successful opening; it continued throughout the entire two-month run. And, not long after closing night, we began our own work sessions again, preparing a new draft for yet another kind of script try-out. This time, we would mount an English-only staged reading, casting mono-lingual actors who didn't know the original. And we would give performances in an Anglo theatre for an all-American audience.

Again, we rewrote during rehearsals and performances, trying to make certain that our words would be valid for actors and audiences who had had no previous encounter with Lorca and no bias toward Hispanic culture.

Because by then, we both knew that we'd stumbled onto something—a way to forge play translations out of the same long process of readings and tryouts and rewrites—that series of crucibles that original scripts must endure and out of which they emerge as playable dramas. It's how most published plays are born. But most published play translations are born not in a trunk, but in lonely nooks deep in the library stacks or as thesis projects for graduate degrees.

It occurred to us that the old stage saw "Plays are not written, they are rewritten" could be applied to play translations. And thanks to BFA and the talent pool of bilingual Hispanic actors in Los Angeles, we had the ideal resources to work with. Applying the process to the plays of Lorca excited us greatly—for here was a splendid playwright who for fifty years had been vastly popular throughout *El Mundo Hispano* and much of the rest of the world, but was almost unknown to general audiences in the English-speaking world.

In Spain, I met with Lorca's sister, Isabel, and with his nephew and literary executor, Manuel Montesinos. They both expressed interest in having better English translations made. And seeing Nuria Espert in her second year of playing "Dona Rosita" to packed houses in Madrid sent me back to California eager to bring more of Lorca's plays into accurate and speakable English.

There have been four, so far, across ten years—all written and rewritten in rehearsal and performance. *Blood Wedding* was even further revised for a Los Angeles revival in 1984 by a greatly developed BFA in a new theatre of its own. It won a cornucopia of awards and went on to tour up and down California. *Yerma* was given a 1933 *Drama-logue* Award for stage writing—the first time a translation had won it. And during the Fiftieth Anniversary Year of Lorca's assassination, the Lorca estate selected our stage-tried translations of the rural trilogy as its authorized versions.

If our work has merit, it is due to the wearisome and enthralling and consummately compulsive process it undergoes. When I described it to that master translator Gregory Rabassa, he seemed to find it all quite logical. Rabassa told me that when working on novels, he declaims every sentence aloud before committing to it. As for plays, he said, "Good dialogue is like a good pair of boots. It takes a little spit to make them shine."

One long, lovely lunch with Rabassa fired me up. BFA's growing reputation and the enthusiasm of its audiences encouraged Carmen. (*La Galban* never needed encouragement—that's what it is to be a *Lorquiana*.) And I should note that our constant requests for foundation grants went unheeded at first, except for the splendid Del Amo Foundation of Los Angeles, whose initial support enabled BFA and the National Repertory Theatre Foundation to commission *Blood Wedding* and mount the first English-language staged reading.

Now the National Endowment for the Arts has given general support to BFA for several years, influences greatly by BFA's ongoing Lorca program. And the Opera/Music Theatre program of NEA has made two grants, enabling us (with Margarita Galban and the composer Ian Krouse) to create an English-language libretto based on Lorca's poetry and plays with a score partly based on his music. Best of all, Bantam Books is bringing out this first collection. We are at work on a second set of three plays.

I dearly hope this publication helps Lorca's fine plays on the path toward their rightful place in our vibrant, pluralistic American culture. That place is on the living stage, where a little spit will make them shine.

But my dearest hope is that reading and seeing Lorca in English will encourage Americans to read his poems and see his plays in their incomparable original Spanish. For me, becoming a *Lorquiano* has been the greatest reward of these past ten years.

Michael Dewell
Los Angeles
April 7, 1987